[redacted]

COMPETITION PONY

COMPETITION PONY

Toni Webber

WARD LOCK LIMITED · LONDON

First published in Great Britain in 1986
by Ward Lock Limited, 8 Clifford Street,
London W1X 1RB, an Egmont Company.

Line drawings by Kevin Maddison

Photographs by Peter Loughran except for p. 148, John Elliot.
The publishers would like to thank Radnage House Riding School, Radnage Bucks for their help with the pictures on pp. 16, 22, 71, 74, 75, 78, 79, 176, 177; they would also like to thank Gary S. Gray for his help with the picture on p. 172.

Text set in Palatino
by J & L Composition Ltd, Filey, N. Yorks

Printed and bound in Italy
by Sagdos

British Library Cataloguing in Publication Data

Webber, Toni
Competition pony.
1. Ponies——Juvenile literature 2. Horsemanship
—Juvenile literature
I. Title
798.2 SF315

ISBN 0-7063-6435-X

Contents

For Charlotte and *her* succession of ponies – Hannibal, Smokey Joe, Bowsy and Minnie – and for Katie, Penny and Lucy and *theirs* – Dusty, Rocky, Snowy, Tammy, Toby, Bowsy, Dillon, Sandy, Andy Pandy, Brandy, Solly, Andy and, of course, Gumboots.

Introduction

A steady, reliable first pony will carry a child happily through the first few years of owning a pony. Unfortunately, ponies do not grow with their owners and a confident twelve-year-old will almost certainly be looking for something with more dash and ability by the time he or she is thirteen.

It is here that first-time pony-owners face a momentous decision, that of making up their minds to find a replacement for what has now become an old friend. It can be a very difficult step to take. If a pony has served you well, it seems an act of terrible disloyalty even to think that it is no longer capable of doing the things you want it to do. But facts must be faced. There is now a wider range of equestrian competitions than ever before from showing classes and affiliated jumping to cross-country and team events, and as their competence increases, most children like to take part.

Similarly, they prefer to join in the competitions their friends are entering. The rosettes displayed on bedroom walls are not a form of boasting but mementoes of great occasions. If you record the date and place of your success on the back of your rosette, together with any other information you can fit in, you have the means of instant recall.

I once overheard a conversation between two friends who were taking down rosettes so that the bedroom of one of them could be redecorated. The whole history of her riding career was there amid the jumble of coloured and faded ribbons.

'That was the day I fell off and the bridle came over his head,' said one, reading the writing on the back of a rosette. 'Oh yes, and that was when we had such an awful judge in the novice jumping,' said her friend 'and Helen jumped the combination *twice*!' Absorbed in so many happy memories, the bedroom took twice as long to prepare as they had expected.

But to enter such action-packed competitions and to win the coveted rosettes, you need a pony that is capable of taking part with credit. This book aims to help you in the transition from your nice, comfortable, grass-fed schoolmaster to a bright and breezy second pony with lots of scope.

It warns you of the pitfalls, the most common of which is to expect too much of a new pony too soon, and, while still recognizing that there are other demands on your time, tells you how to get and to keep your pony in a fit condition. It describes the sort of stabling you may now need and the routine required to safeguard your pony's welfare and happiness.

Parents are not forgotten. Behind every child competing regularly and successfully in all types of competition, there is an ever-willing mother or an obliging father prepared to sacrifice her or his own time and interests. Sacrifice is perhaps the wrong word; most parents become as enthusiastic as their children and, while not quite ready actually to sit on the pony themselves, will undertake most other tasks, even tack-cleaning. A chapter in this book looks at the role of the parent, particularly with regard to transport and costs.

As for you, by the time you are ready for a second pony, you are entering into the most enjoyable period of your riding career. Whether or not you intend in the future to earn your living by working with horses, a good choice of competition pony now will lay the foundation for a lifelong interest in horses, a love of their beauty and a true appreciation of their value as a companion and friend.

Toni Webber

CHAPTER 1
Choosing a competition pony

Sooner or later, the time will come when you have grown out of your first pony. The reason may be purely physical – a long-legged thirteen-year-old looks silly on a 12 hh pony – but, far more likely, you are now capable of doing much more than your pony is.

You will, for example, be entering a variety of competitions, from gymkhana classes to cross-country events. You will reach an age when the fences in the jumping events open to you are too high for your little pony, and although he is quite able to carry your weight out hacking he does not have the scope for anything more ambitious.

The moment of decision comes around the age of twelve or thirteen. At twelve, you are still eligible for most minimus jumping classes or for the 12.2 hh and under junior jumping and showing events. Once you reach thirteen, however, the only showing class left open to you if you have a small pony is the working hunter pony under 13 hh.

Most children try to put off the decision as long as possible, especially if their first pony has given them faithful service for many years. Some children are able to pass the pony on to a younger brother or sister; a few decide to keep him just for gymkhana and handy pony events. But for those who cannot afford to keep more than one pony at a time, a new home must be found for the first pony and a search started for the second.

FINDING A COMPETITION PONY

Competition ponies are found in exactly the same way as first ones: through word of mouth, advertisements in horse magazines, dealers, or at auctions. But you do have an advantage over those far-off days when you first acquired a pony of your own. You probably know people through the Pony Club and local shows, and it will be much easier to spread the word around that you are looking for a pony. You probably also have a better idea of the sort of pony you are looking for.

Someone older than you may be in much the same position as you are, ready to sell their pony and move on to something bigger, but reluctant to do so because they are anxious to find a good home. The knowledge that you are in the market could just be the factor that encourages them to approach you. Similarly, someone else might come to you and ask if you would sell your present pony. A great many transactions take place without the ponies concerned ever being advertised at all.

It is, of course, important to decide exactly what type of pony you want. If you still enjoy gymkhana games but are beginning to get a taste for show-jumping or cross-country courses, then you must find an all-round pony – one which is nimble enough to nip in and out of bending poles, but bold enough to tackle a drop fence, a big spread or to go through water with confidence. Perhaps you like the discipline of dressage and would prefer a suitable one-day eventer or a combined training specialist. Or perhaps you

When the time comes to get a new pony, you must think carefully about what kind of pony you want. If you are developing a taste for show-jumping and cross-country courses, you will need a pony who can tackle fences confidently.

fancy the idea of all these competitions but have been frustrated so far by the limitations of your present pony.

People have mixed feelings about buying a known pony from their own area. On the one hand, you have the advantage of knowing what a pony can do, and forewarning of all its habits. On the other hand, there is the possibility that you might not get on as well with the pony as its current owner does. There is nothing more shattering to one's self-confidence than to overhear someone saying, 'Of course, that pony did terribly well when Angela had him; can't think what's happened to him now,' just when you have completed a dreadful show-jumping round and are beginning to wonder the same thing yourself.

If you buy a pony from another part of the country, the chances are that no one locally knows his reputation. If you do well, you can take much of the credit yourself; if you do badly, you have not lost face.

Unless you have contacts, such as friends or relations, in a distant part of the country, the best place to find a new pony is through magazine advertisements. An advertisement will give the pony's height and age. It will also state the activities that the pony has taken part in or been successful at.

Standard abbreviations are used in advertisements to describe these activities, and you should be familiar with them. They are listed in Appendix III page 93. Remember that the greater the pony's achievements, the higher his price is likely to be.

In addition to describing the pony's achievements the advertisement will emphasize a pony's good points; for example, quiet to box, shoe, clip, and so on. Sometimes, the phrase 'Not a novice ride' is included and this, of course, is open to various interpretations. It could mean that the pony is lively and needs firm handling but is generally viceless; or that it is liable to belt off at the least provocation, has a mouth like leather and needs someone with enormous strength to keep it even half-way under control. You cannot tell which category applies until you try out the pony and, even then, you should ask the sellers to explain exactly what they mean. Never forget that while people may put only half-truths in an advertisement, it is difficult for them to tell a downright lie if asked a direct question.

What you are no doubt looking for in your second pony is a bigger, faster and more capable replica of the one that you have already. Forget it! Every pony is different, and each time you buy one you are buying a unique individual, with his own temperament and characteristics. You will have to get to know him just as you got to know your first pony.

Many riders expect to get on a new pony and have him perform as well as he did with his previous owner. However, a relationship between pony and rider does not develop overnight; it may be six months or more before the two of you are going well together.

Sometimes, it is true, the transition from one owner to the next is smooth and trouble-free. On the other hand, you may find that it goes well to begin with and then, for no obvious reason, things go wrong. The pony develops a tendency to stop or run out at a jump; instead of being lively and on the bit, he falls behind; he may take charge when you are out on a ride, or suddenly decide that he can't go without company.

There may be a number of reasons for the change. Perhaps you have altered his diet – try increasing his intake of energy-producing food; perhaps he has developed a liking for another pony in the field and gets upset if he has to go anywhere without him. Most probably, the reason is that you do not ride the pony exactly as his previous owner did. If your last pony had only to be pointed at a jump in order to jump it, you probably think that is how all ponies should be ridden round a jumping course. You have forgotten that some ponies need to be told exactly how to tackle a fence, the speed they should go at, and the moment of take-off. If your last pony rushed his fences and had to be held back until the final moment it is no good using the same method with a pony that loses impulsion if he is checked at the wrong time.

Some ponies are naturally confident. Others take their cue from their rider. If you think as you approach a jump, 'That looks big; we'll never get over it,' your pony may sense your feelings and believe that you know best. Result: a refusal. Why should he jump something that even his rider is frightened of?

At this stage, it is more important than ever that you should continue to take regular riding lessons. An experienced instructor will be able to tell you where you are going wrong and help you to put things right.

SELLING YOUR OLD PONY

Whether you sell your pony locally to friends or acquaintances, or to strangers who live far away, depends on how much you mind seeing your pony in someone else's care.

The advantage of a local sale is that you will already know something about the pony's new home and can feel confident that he will be properly looked after. If you sell him to strangers, you must face up to the fact that he is going out of your life, probably for ever.

Many people worry that if they advertise the pony he may end up on the meat market. Obviously, there is no guarantee that the man who buys your pony and tells you that it is a present for his daughter is not a slaughter-man, but you can take some steps to check where your pony is going.

For example, once the sale has been agreed, insist that the pony is not collected until, say, the following week, or if your family has a trailer, offer to deliver the pony yourselves. In the meantime, visit the new home, if it is within reasonable distance, and check on the conditions he will be living in. If you have friends in the area, ask if they know of the family concerned. People quickly acquire a reputation – whether good or bad – in the horse world.

You are perfectly entitled to ask the would-be purchasers if they have ever owned a pony before, but there is no need to be put off by those who admit inexperience. After all, you were in that situation yourself once. Ask whether the new owner is a member of the Pony Club, and urge them to join if they have not already done so. You can also ask to visit the pony from time to time. No genuine buyer would object to that.

It is up to you whether you sell your pony with all his tack or not. If you are getting a bigger pony, there is probably no reason to keep the first pony's saddle and bridle, and at least you would know that he will be wearing tack that fits him.

Some people always have the pony shod before the sale and bring his inoculations and worming up to date. That way, they can be sure that they have done the very best for the pony.

The day he leaves is bound to be a sad one, especially if you have had him for a long time. But once you have grown out of a pony, it is not a good idea to keep him purely for sentimental reasons. Ponies are happiest when they are working, in a home where they are loved and cared for. Your pony's new owners should be able to give him all the attention which you, with your next pony, might not have time for.

LENDING A PONY

It has become a common practice nowadays to let a pony go out on loan rather than to sell him. Provided you do not need the cash which selling him would produce, it is quite a good method by which your pony can lead a useful life without your having to say goodbye to him altogether.

Before lending the pony, make certain that you and his new 'owner' have agreed on all the details of the arrangement. Decide beforehand who is to be responsible for the feed bills, vet's bills, farrier's fees, and so on. Decide on the period of the loan. Sometimes it is better to fix a limit of, say, two years than to let the pony go for an indefinite time.

Make a list of everything that you are sending with him: saddle, including girths and stirrup-irons and leathers, bridle, head-collar, lead-rope, and so on. Settle which of you is to make the ultimate decision should the pony have an accident or become so ill that he has to be humanely destroyed. Do bear in mind that such a decision sometimes has to be made very quickly. A pony should not have to suffer longer than necessary because you are away on holiday and cannot be contacted.

When you have agreed the terms, write them down. Prepare two copies of the agreement and get the signatures of both parties on each copy.

Then let your pony go with a light heart. You have a new pony now to focus your love and attention on.

CHAPTER 2

Stabling

When you progress to a second pony, and especially if you intend to enter competitions, the question arises as to the best method of keeping him. Your previous pony lived out all the year round. When you went to gymkhanas, you caught him early in the morning, groomed him as best you could, spent the day at the show and turned him out in his field again in the evening.

The system worked very well and your pony remained healthy. His thick winter coat protected him during the winter months, and the field shelter gave him relief from the flies and hot sun in summer. Of course, he did tend to sweat up a little in the winter, especially when you took him to the Pony Club meet, and it was often annoying on gymkhana days to find a wet pony in the field when it had rained the night before. But at the level of competitions you were tackling, none of this really mattered. In any case, it was the same for everyone.

Now you have a new pony, and you are becoming more ambitious. When you go to a show, you want your pony to look immaculate. The last thing you want is a grey coat disfigured by grass stains or a tail clogged with burrs. A stable can prevent this. Your pony will still spend most of his time out-of-doors, but you can bring him in for the night before a show. In winter, you can have him partially clipped and keep him in at night and out by day. You can regulate his intake of food much more closely.

This is the time to consider building a stable or converting an outbuilding into a loose box. If your parents are willing to buy a ready-made stable, collect as much information as you can so that you can tell them exactly what you need. There are a number of manufacturers of sectional stables, and most of them advertise in the horse magazines. They will send you pamphlets and price lists on request, and by comparing the various designs, you will be able to form an idea of your own requirements.

The most basic form of stable available is a simple loose box fitted with a pitched roof, window and divided door. In some designs, the front of the roof is extended to form an overhang which helps to shelter the stable from rain and sun. It is essential that the stable has good guttering, but kicking boards lining the inside walls are necesarry only if your pony is going to spend much of his time in the stable.

Prices include delivery and erection but not the preparation of the site. You will have to make separate arrangements to lay down a concrete base. Whether planning permission is needed or not depends on your local authority, but a visit to the local planning office will provide all the necessary information.

If you are hoping, in due course, to buy a horse, it is sensible to get a loose box big enough for a hunter. The ideal size is 4.3 × 3.6 m (14 × 12 ft), which gives a big horse plenty of room to move around in. For a pony, 3.6 × 3 m (12 × 10 ft) would be ample. Much, however, depends on what you can afford.

If a pony is in a stable all day, it is important that he can look out and watch whatever is going on in the yard.

The stable should not open towards the prevailing wind. South or south-east would probably be best, especially if the roof has an overhang.

The conversion of an existing outbuilding is a cheaper alternative to starting from scratch. Many older houses have a brick-built garage or shed which is not being used for a car, and as the following example shows these can be converted into a stable without too much trouble. The existing building had three brick walls beneath a pitched roof and a large, sliding, wooden door across the front. The door provided enough material to make a fourth wall over one half of the open side and a properly hung, divided stable door to fit the other half. The existing concrete floor was in good condition and already had a small groove, which would provide drainage. Some parts of the brick walls were repointed. The stable was finished off with a coat of dark brown paint on the lower half of the inside walls and a coat of white paint on the upper half. Although the stable has no window, the white paint inside makes it light and airy; the darker paint below makes it easier to keep clean.

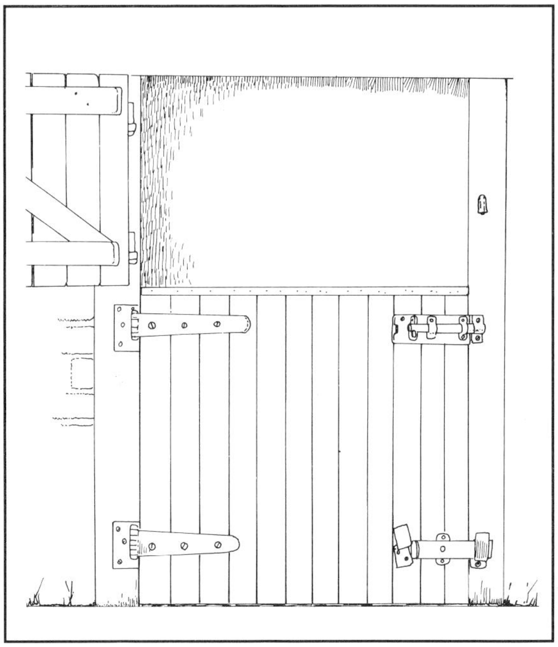

A stable door should be divided, so that the top half can be left open to provide ventilation. The bottom half needs bolts top and bottom to be really secure as many ponies learn to undo any bolts they can reach.

STABLE FITTINGS

A loose box needs very few fittings. The most important, of course, are rings to which you can tie either haynets or the pony. These need to be bolted right through the wall to be completely secure. A manger is useful, but it should be removable so that it can be cleaned out from time to time. Bucket holders can be bought, but an old car tyre is just as effective for preventing a bucket of water or feed from being knocked over.

Doors should be secured with bolts. The bottom door needs two bolts, of which the lower one should be a kick bolt that can be operated with the foot. One bolt is sufficient for the top door. Both doors need hooks and staples to hold them back when they are wide open. The doorway should be at least 1.25 m (4 ft) wide so that a horse or pony can pass through without banging himself. The doors should open outwards.

If your stable is fitted with electric lighting – and it is extremely useful to have safe, artificial lighting available – ensure that the bulb is well out of reach of the pony. A bulkhead light is best for a wall-fitting. For safety's sake, the switch should be outside the stable; a properly insulated, exterior light-switch is best.

If you use a hay-rack rather than a haynet, do not fix it to the wall above the height of the pony's head. The old-fashioned system of high-level hay-racks is now regarded as uncomfortable for the horse and even dangerous, because of the risk of hay seeds and dust falling into his eyes.

BEDDING

When a pony is to spend a night in a stable he will need some form of bedding. Wood-shavings and straw are the two most popular forms, but peat moss is a good alternative.

Wood-shavings These are usually sold compressed into plastic-covered bales. They are easy to stack and, provided the plastic has not split, can be stored out-of-doors. Some firms sell the shavings more loosely packed in hessian sacks, but these need to be covered over if they are kept in the open air. Compressed shavings need separating out with a fork or by hand so that they do not form a lumpy bed; the loose shavings only need raking over.

Shavings are sometimes combined with sawdust for economy, in which case the sawdust is put down first. Always cover any drains in the stable before putting down sawdust, so that they do not get clogged up. When raking over sawdust and shavings, check that they do not contain old nails or sharp off-cuts of wood which might harm your pony.

Straw The best type of straw for bedding is *wheat straw,* because it is warm and comfortable and drains well. It is usually quite easy and cheap to obtain. *Oat straw* is more porous and therefore gets wet and soggy quite quickly. Ponies do tend to eat it, however, just as they will *barley straw,* although the latter makes good bedding provided it has been made by a combine harvester and is free of prickly awns.

Peat moss This tends to be dusty when it is first laid but it is less of a fire hazard than straw or shavings. It needs to be raked regularly to prevent it from becoming hard-packed.

Bedding is necessary in a stable not only to give the pony a soft surface to lie down on, but also to provide insulation and to prevent the pony's legs from being jarred through standing on a hard floor.

Care of bedding

When a pony has spent a few hours in a stable, some of his bedding will have become wet and soiled. This must be replaced by fresh material.

With a straw bed, the old clean straw should be separated from the rest and piled in a corner. After the dirty straw has been taken away, sweep the floor and allow it to air before re-laying the bed and adding new straw.

With shavings and moss, the droppings and wet patches are forked into a wheelbarrow or skip and the bedding raked to keep it sweet.

Laying a bed

It is a false economy to stint on the amount of bedding used. As a pony moves round his stable, the bedding will be shifted about. If it was very sparse to start with, this will produce bare patches of floor, with the risk to the pony of capped hocks or elbows from lying on concrete. So make the bed as thickly as you can. Shake up the straw to make it springy and comfortable and pile a double layer around the edges as a precaution against injury and draughts. Shavings and peat moss should also be piled higher against the walls.

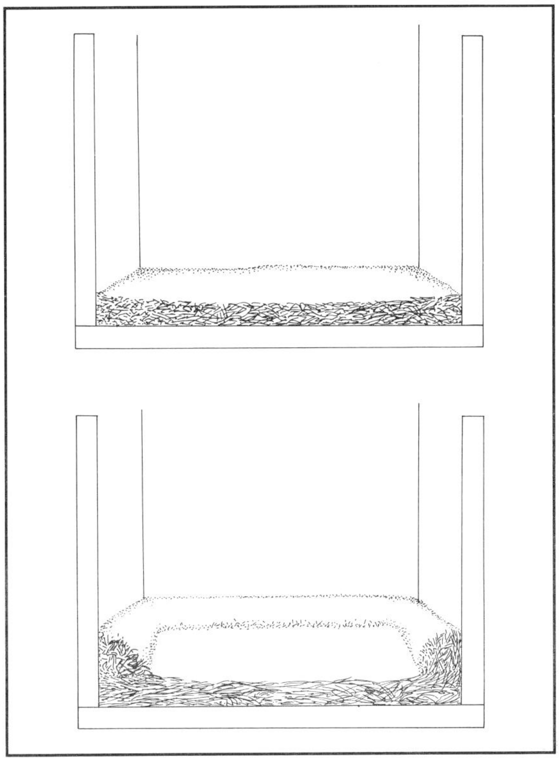

The wrong and the right way of laying a straw bed. **Top:** incorrect. **Bottom:** correct. The straw has been banked around the edges to protect the pony from draughts and risk of injury.

If your time is limited, you can use the *deep litter* system. Only the droppings are removed each time and fresh material is added to the existing bed. In time, the bed will become very deep and eventually, say every three to four months, you will have to take out the whole lot and begin again. However, removing the entire bed from a stable which has been in regular use for about fifteen weeks is a heavy task.

If you will not be using the stable very often, you should re-do the bed on each occasion. While the stable is empty, heap the existing, unsoiled bedding into one corner and leave the floor clean and aired.

KEEPING A PONY IN AT NIGHT

If you plan to work your pony quite hard during the winter, hunting regularly or taking him to indoor shows, it is sensible to have him partially clipped, so that he will not sweat up too much when he is working, and to keep him in by night and out by day. The dark evenings will prevent you from exercising him during the week, but he will get enough exercise for himself if he is in a field by day. You can ensure that he is warm and well fed at night by bringing him into the stable when you get home from school. Remember to keep the top half of the stable door open at all times.

There is usually no need to start this routine until winter arrives, but once you have started it you will have to carry on until the following April. If there are likely to be any problems – if your pony's field, for example, is a long way from his loose box – it is better to keep him turned out permanently and provide him with a field shelter, rather than to use a stable.

Depending on the clip you choose (see page 53), it may be necessary to put the pony in a New Zealand rug whenever he is turned out in a field. An unclipped pony or one with a belly clip only, will not require either a New Zealand rug or a night rug.

The combined system – field by day, stable by night – takes up more time than if you visit your pony in his field to feed him. The stable has to be mucked out and the new bed laid, and if this has to be done in daylight hours, you may find that your winter timetable gets very rushed. Whether you get the stable ready in the morning or wait until after school depends on how good you are at getting up early. On the whole, it is probably easier to muck out in the morning, and the before-school routine need not take more than fifteen or twenty minutes.

Firstly, take some hay out to the pony's field (for quantity, see page 25): you can give it either in a haynet or spread on the ground. Then return to the stable, remove the pony's night rug (if he wears one) and pick out his feet. Put his New Zealand rug on him, and turn him into the field. Return to the stable again, remove all the soiled straw or shavings to the muck-heap and prepare the new bed. Fill the night's haynets and hang up. Empty and rinse out the water buckets and refill. Hang the night rug in a dry, airy place, say goodbye to your pony, and get back to breakfast and school.

The longest job is the mucking out of the stable. If you can manage to complete this in the morning, all you have to do in the evening is to prepare the pony's short feed, swap his rugs over and put him into his box for the night. That takes up very little time and you should have no difficulty in fitting it into after-school activities, such as extra work, music lessons or club meetings.

DISPOSAL OF MANURE

Well-rotted stable manure is a blessing to gardeners. If you keep a well-ordered muck-heap, you will be able to sell bags of compost, which provides a handy source of pocket-money. If possible, build your heap on a concrete base and preferably make two bays so that one can be left to rot while you are filling the other. A proprietary compost maker can be added to encourage decomposition. Straw rots down more quickly than wood-shavings.

CHAPTER 3

Stable routine

It is the daily routine which really brings home the difference between owning a pony and owning a horse. Most ponies are kept at grass most of the time, although they may be stabled at night in the winter. Bringing a pony in from his field after school, turning him out the next morning and mucking out his loose box once a day, take up perhaps one hour in twenty-four. To look after a horse that is permanently stabled, including grooming and exercise, occupies a large part of the daylight hours. Unless you intend to make a career with horses, when doing your own horse may be part of your training, you will almost certainly have to fit all this in around your time at school or college, although you may be able to share the duties with a friend or a member of your family.

As horses are creatures of habit, you must work out a timetable and stick to it as closely as possible. Feeding times should not be varied at all except on special days, such as when hunting or showing. A horse seems to know his feeding time, to the minute, and if you are late he will begin to fret, stamping his feet, pawing the ground, kicking the door and the sides of his box, perhaps even picking up bad habits like crib-biting.

Draw up your timetable carefully as soon as you get your new horse. The following will remind you what has to be done. You can, of course, alter the times to suit yourself.

A DAILY TIMETABLE

7.00 a.m. Enter the stable, put headcollar on horse and tie him up, so that you can inspect him carefully for any overnight injury.

Empty the water bucket, rinse out and refill. Offer the fresh water to the horse but do not worry if he does not want a drink.

Refill the haynet and tie it up.

Muck out the stable, removing all soiled straw and droppings. Leave the clean straw in a pile in one corner. If you use shavings, remove droppings and cut out any wet patches. Rake the bed level.

Pick out the horse's feet. If he is quiet, you can pick out each foot in turn straight into the skep, which prevents the pickings from littering the stable floor. Remove the skep or sweep up the pickings.

Quarter the horse; that is, give him a perfunctory grooming. Use a sponge to clean the eyes, nostrils and dock. Unbuckle the front of his night rug and fold it back over the surcingle or roller. Use a body brush lightly on his head, neck, chest and forelegs. Refasten the rug. Then fold back the rear of the rug and brush the horse's hindquarters. Use a water brush or sponge to get rid of any night stains. Replace the rug. Finish off by brushing out the mane and tail.

(7 a.m. cont.)
Lay the day bed by using the clean straw piled in the corner.
Prepare the horse's feed.

7.45 a.m. Give the horse his feed and leave him to eat in peace while you have your own breakfast.

9.30 a.m. Remove droppings from the stable.
Take off the night rug and tack up. Take the horse out for at least an hour's exercise. When you return, remove the saddle and bridle. Give your horse time to roll.

11 a.m. Short rack: that is, tie up the horse fairly short so that he cannot move about.
Give him a thorough groom (strapping). This should be done within twenty minutes of returning from exercise, as it is best carried out when the horse is warm and the pores of the skin are open. He should, however, be dry. If he sweats a lot during exercise you should give him time to dry off.
Strapping starts with picking out the feet. This is followed by a good going over with the dandy-brush to remove dirt and sweat. Always brush in the same direction as the lie of the coat and complete the near side before moving to the off side. Pay special attention to the saddle mark and girth area, hocks, knees, fetlocks and pasterns.
Take the body brush, push the mane to the wrong side and tackle the roots of the mane, removing all scurf and dust. Finish by bringing the mane back to the right side and brushing it carefully, working from withers to poll. Brush the forelock.
Now go over the body with the body brush, putting plenty of weight into the brushing movements. Use a circular motion, but finish in the direction of the coat, and give a slight outward flick at the end of each brush stroke to

(11 a.m. cont.)
force dirt and dust away from the body. Use a curry-comb to clean the body brush as you go.
Groom the head with the body brush. If the headcollar gets in the way, take it off and refasten it round the horse's neck.
Use the body brush on the tail, removing any tangles with the fingers.
Finish off by strapping the body thoroughly with a wisp. This action tones up the muscular parts of the body. It hardens the muscles, stimulates the oil-producing glands, improves the blood supply to the skin and brings a shine to the coat. A wisp is made from soft hay, twisted to form a rope. When the rope is about 3 m (10 ft) long, form two

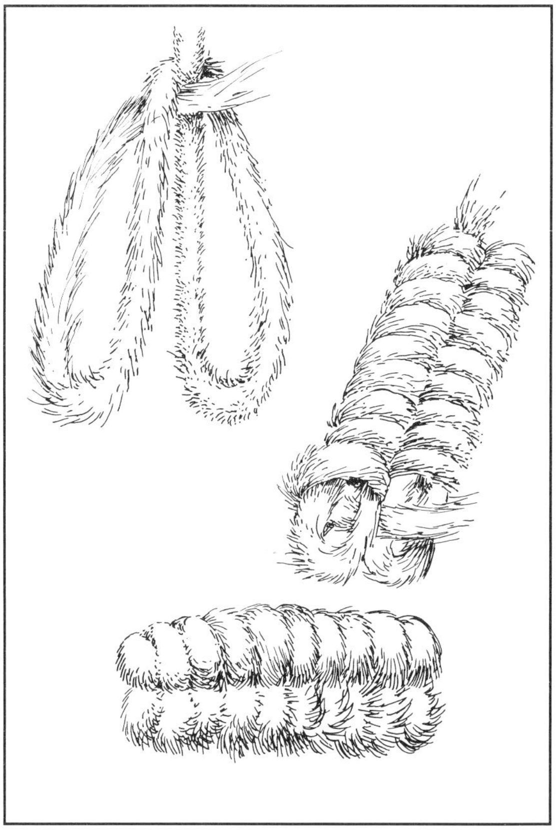

The three stages of making a wisp from a rope of a soft, twisted hay

(11 a.m. cont.)
loops at one end of it. Wind the remaining hay-rope round both loops together and finish off by passing the loose end through the loops and pulling tight. Beat the wisp on the ground, stamp on it or bang it against a wall, to flatten it. The finished wisp should not disintegrate as you use it. Effective use of the wisp requires practice and knowledge of where it will do the most good. The wisp is needed on the muscular parts of the body; the neck, the sides of the shoulders and on the quarters and thighs. Put plenty of effort into banging it hard against the horse's body, following the lie of the coat, and avoid the loins and bony parts. When you have finished the near side move round and give the off side the same treatment–and then take a short rest, because you should be feeling exhausted.

Fortunately, the next stage, by comparison, is quite restful. Using a sponge and clean water, wash around the eyelids, removing any mucus which may have collected in the corners of the eyes. Rinse the sponge out, squeeze and wipe over the lips and muzzle. Rinse once more and wipe the nostrils. Complete the washing process by sponging the dock and the underside of the tail.

Finish off the mane by using the water brush, dipped in water and shaken to remove the surplus, to smooth the hair into place.

Wash the feet (unless the weather is too cold), carefully removing any mud, and taking care not to let any water get into the hollow of the heel. If you do accidentally wet it, take care to dry it properly. If there is any sign of cracked heels or mud fever–soreness, redness of the skin (particularly noticeable on white feet)

(11 a.m. cont.)
or raw patches–dust with an antibiotic powder. Petroleum jelly, liberally smeared around the heels and over the pastern and fetlock joint, will give protection.

When the feet have dried, brush hoof oil all over the outside of the hoof wall as high as the coronet.

Use a stable rubber over the whole coat to give a last polish. Then put the day rug on the horse.

Refill the water buckets, and untie the horse. Prepare the midday feed.

12.30 p.m. Give the mid-day feed.

Refill haynet.

Tidy up the yard.

4.00 p.m. Tie up the horse and pick out his feet. Use the skep to remove droppings and shake up the bedding.

Refill water buckets.

Untie horse and prepare third feed.

4.45 p.m. Give the third feed.

7.00 p.m. Tie up the horse.

Remove droppings in skep and lay the night bed, adding enough clean, well-shaken straw to make a soft, springy bed. Make certain that the straw is well banked around the sides of the box.

Refill water buckets and haynet.

Remove day rug, and give the horse a final grooming, called setting fair. Brush him lightly all over with the body brush, and use the wisp on his muscles.

Put the night rug on him, adding a blanket underneath if the night is likely to be very cold. It is better to give the horse extra clothing to keep him warm and to leave the top half of the stable door open, than to shut the top door. Untie the horse.

Prepare the last feed.

Page 22 A bright, friendly, cheerful stable yard, which is neat and clean. Heads over the stable doors show that the horses here take an interest in everything that is going on.

7.30 p.m. Give the final feed.

8.30 p.m. Clean the tack, unless you have managed to fit it in during the afternoon.

10.00 p.m. Visit the stable to check that all is well. Do not go right into the stable unless the rugs have slipped and need adjusting. You should disturb the horse as little as possible.

It is obvious from the timetable that looking after a horse can be a full-time job. If you are at school or college, or are at work all day, you will certainly need a friend to help you, although there are short cuts that you can take. Grooming, for example, need not be quite so thorough, but feeding times and exercise must not be varied or skimped.

EXERCISE

Exercise for the horse can be difficult to arrange, especially in winter when it may be dark before you leave the house and after you return. You may be able to arrange to have the use of an all-weather school; fitted with floodlights if possible. An indoor school is even better, as you can then exercise at any time and in any weather. But whether it is an outdoor, floodlit manege or an indoor one, you must be able to get to it without having to do any roadwork after dark.

If there is no way in which you can exercise your horse in safety or in daylight, the only solution is to turn him out during the day. A small exercising paddock would be sufficient for him to exercise himself. Even a securely-fenced schooling arena, with a bark or wood-chip surface, is better than leaving the horse to stand all day long in a loose box. A clipped horse can be rugged up against the weather. Choose the best New Zealand rug that you can afford; if possible try to buy a self-righting one without a surcingle. Put an extra blanket underneath if the weather is very cold.

STABLE VICES

A horse that is left all day in a loose box without any form of exercise runs all sorts of risks, from filled legs to boredom. Boredom leads to stable vices, which, once established, are very difficult to cure.

The stable vice known as weaving. The horse swings his head from side to side.

One method of preventing weaving is to suspend a brick over the stable door.

Kicking the panelling

This annoying habit is disturbing to other horses, and to your neighbours if your stable is near other houses. It is dangerous, as the horse might injure himself in the process. And it is expensive if the panels have to be repaired regularly.

Weaving

The horse moves his head from side to side, often shifting his weight in a rocking movement from one foot to another. It is a common vice, and causes problems because the horse is using up energy and can lose weight as a result. Sometimes, the horse likes to have his head over the stable door while he is weaving. A grille or bars fitted over the opening may discourage him. The cause is nearly always lack of exercise and boredom. More exercise or a change of scenery could cure it altogether.

Crib-biting

The horse takes hold of the edge of the stable door or manger with his teeth, sucks in air and swallows it. It is damaging to the horse because it causes indigestion and loss of condition. It is almost always a result of boredom, although a horse can develop the habit by watching and copying another horse. One possible remedy is to wrap sheet metal over the top of the door. However, this is only a deterrent and it may not work. If the habit has not become established, turn the horse out into a field and he may forget about it. However, crib-biters will use the top of the gate or a fencing post to suck in air.

Crib-biting is another stable vice. The horse takes hold of the top of the door, or any suitable ledge, and sucks in air.

Wind-sucking

This is similar to crib-biting, except that the horse does not have to take hold of anything in order to swallow air. He simply arches his neck and draws in his chin. Unless you can cure the boredom, it is very difficult to cure a confirmed wind-sucker.

Some vets advocate a small operation to cure both wind-sucking and crib-biting which has been very successful. This involves making a small hole through the flesh of each cheek, which prevents the horse from creating a vacuum in his mouth.

CHAPTER 4
Feeding

Hay should always form the major portion of a pony's winter diet, whatever work he is doing. It may also be necessary to feed hay in a very hot summer when the available grass has dried up and turned brown.

Hay alone, however, will not provide sufficient energy for a pony taking part regularly in shows, gymkhanas, hunting, or Pony Club activities. The feeding programme should then include some combination of concentrates.

Most diet sheets for ponies and horses are worked out in relation to the animal's body weight, and weight is also used to measure the quantity of food to be given. The winter feed table below gives a rough guide to a pony's needs, but it is open to a number of variations as no two ponies' requirements are exactly the same.

Getting the diet right for your own pony will depend on trial and error. If, for example, your pony appears to be losing weight, although he is healthy in all other respects and his worming programme is up to date, his intake of concentrates will have to be stepped up. If he is lively, choose a food such as barley that puts on flesh without making him excitable. If he seems to 'run out of puff' quite quickly, give him some extra oats.

Introduce changes in his diet gradually and be guided as far as possible by the pony himself. If his haynet is emptied between one feeding time and the next, he may be getting too little. As far as hay is concerned it is always better to offer too much. A spring balance hanging in your feed room will give you an accurate reading of the amount of hay you are offering.

When measuring dry feeds, use scales to weigh the quantity contained in, say, one

Winter feed table for a pony wholly at grass or stabled by night

Pony's height	Hay	Concentrates
Under 11 hh	2.2–3.6 kg (5–8 lb)	Cubes 450 g (1 lb) Bran 225 g (∂ lb) Sugar-beet 225 g (∂ lb)
11–12.2 hh	3.6–4.5 kg (8–10 lb)	Cubes 900 g (2 lb) Bran 450 g (1 lb) Sugar-beet 450 g (1 lb)
12.3–13.2 hh	4.5–5.4 kg (10–12 lb)	Cubes 1.4 kg (3 lb) Bran 450 g (1 lb) Sugar-beet 700 g (1∂ lb)
13.3–14.2 hh	5.4–6.4 kg (12–14 lb)	Cubes 1.8 kg (4 lb) Bran 450 g (1 lb) Sugar-beet 900 g (2 lb)

heaped scoopful. Provided you always use the same scoop, there is no need to weigh accurately each time, but do not be tempted to give a little more for luck.

Sugar-beet, either as pulp or as cubes, should be weighed dry, but it must be soaked for twelve to twenty-four hours before being fed. Oats may be substituted for cubes but the quantity of oats should be less. Allow 450 g (1 lb) of oats for 700 g ($1\frac{1}{2}$ lb) of cubes. Other forms of concentrate may be substituted according to your pony's tastes, but try not to exceed the total quantity by weight for each feed. Root crops and apples are always popular with ponies and can be added to the feed at any time.

CONCENTRATES

Cubes

There are various types of cubes on the market. They contain a mixture of many ingredients, including vitamins. The manufacturer's leaflet will tell you what the cubes contain and you should follow the maker's recommendation for your particular pony. Some cubes, for example, contain more protein than others and a high protein cube could be dangerous for your pony. Most ponies like cubes, but you should always mix them with dampened bran or chaff before giving them to your pony. This will ensure that he eats slowly, digesting them properly. Never buy too much at one time as cubes will deteriorate in store. Storage time: approximately three months. Cubes are a good feed for ponies as they are less heating than oats.

Oats

This is the traditional food for horses. Good oats have large, hard, clean grains. They may be fed whole but are more easily digested if they are bruised, rolled or crushed. However, crushed oats can go stale quite quickly and should be used within three to four weeks. Chaff or bran should be mixed with the oats before feeding. Oats can make ponies quite excitable and should therefore be fed to ponies with care.

Barley

This is a very good winter food for ponies kept at grass, as it keeps them fat and well without getting them hotted up. Whole barley grains have a very hard and indigestible covering which must be broken down before being fed to horses. If you buy rolled, crushed or flaked barley, or pre-cooked (micronized) barley, this will already have been done.

If you buy whole-grain barley, it must be simmered in water for four to six hours to soften the grains before you feed it to your pony. If whole grains pass out in the droppings, the barley is not being cooked for long enough. This is an inconvenient way of feeding barley. It is tedious, and it creates an unpleasant smell while it is cooking. However, it is an excellent feed for fattening thin horses, and for tempting poor eaters.

Flaked maize

This should always be used sparingly as, although it is good for fattening purposes, it can overheat the pony's blood. It is often an ingredient in proprietary mixtures and other combined feeds. Although in the UK maize is always fed flaked, in the USA it is fed whole or on the cob.

Beans

Dried beans are nutritious, but are considered too heating for ponies. A small handful mixed with the pony's other feed may be beneficial in winter if the pony lives out. Beans are usually bruised or split before feeding. If in doubt, it is best to leave beans out of your pony's diet.

Sugar-beet

Dried sugar-beet is sold as pulp or as cubes and it provides both energy and roughage. It is an excellent winter feed for ponies that are kept mainly at grass, and is always very popular with them. *It is essential to soak dried sugar-beet before use.* Place the pulp or cubes in a bucket and add water at the rate of approximately $2\frac{1}{2}$ parts water to 1 part pulp, or 4 parts water to 1 part cubes. Soak for twelve to twenty-four hours. Never soak more sugar-beet than will be fed. Sugar-beet starts to ferment as soon as it is mixed with water and the fermentation must not be allowed to continue for too long. After soaking, always pour away any surplus liquid before mixing with chaff, bran and other feeds.

Dry sugar-beet should never be fed to a pony. It swells considerably on contact with water or other liquids, and it would be dangerous if this happened in the pony's stomach. Take care to keep dried sugar-beet cubes away from other cubes to avoid muddling them up.

Bran
This is made from wheat-husk. The most suitable type for ponies is known as broad bran. It should smell fresh and be free of lumps. Its main purpose is to give bulk to the feed and to encourage the pony to eat slowly. It should be dampened before being fed. Wet bran has a laxative effect on horses, dry bran the reverse.

Bran-mash
This is a good pick-me-up for a tired pony or one that is off-colour. It is made by filling a bucket about three-quarters full of bran and adding boiling water until the bran is thoroughly wet. The bucket should then be covered with a thick cloth or hessian sack and left to 'cook' slowly while it cools. Once it is cool enough for the pony to eat, stir in about 55 g (2 oz) of salt, a few oats or some crushed barley, and a spoonful of molasses or black treacle, diluted in warm water.

Oatmeal gruel
This is another useful tonic for a tired pony after a hard day's work, provided the pony will take it. Simply put a double handful of oatmeal into a bucket, and add enough boiling water to make a thin gruel. Stir well. Leave it to cool. It should be thin enough for the pony to drink.

Linseed
As a general conditioner and means of making the coat shine, linseed would be hard to beat. Its drawback is that it takes a while to prepare. It has to be cooked properly as raw linseed is poisonous to horses. If you wish to improve your pony's coat during the winter, linseed can be made into a jelly and added to the feed once a week. To make the jelly, put 110–225 g (4–8 oz) of linseed in a saucepan, cover it with water and leave the pan in a warm place, such as a very cool oven, until the next day. Then add more water and bring to the boil. Allow it to boil for ten to fifteen minutes before taking the saucepan from the heat and leaving it to cool. As it cools, the linseed sets into a *jelly*, which you mix with your pony's feed. It is very important that the water containing the linseed should boil. If you add extra water at the second stage, but still bring it to the boil, the result will be linseed *tea*, which can be mixed with bran to make a linseed mash.

Chaff
This is simply hay, sometimes mixed with a small quantity of oat straw, which has been passed through a giant mincing machine and chopped into small pieces. It is sometimes called chop for that reason. The mincing machine or 'chaff cutter' is a useful piece of equipment for stables with several horses, but it is not worth the expense if you have only one or two ponies to look after. Instead, ready-prepared chaff can usually be bought from a corn merchant. The purpose of chaff is to add bulk to a short feed, encouraging the pony to eat more slowly. Some greedy ponies gobble their food so quickly that some of the nutritional value is lost.

Mixtures
There are various ready-mixed foods on the market and they are quite useful for ponies which do not like cubes. They look like breakfast food and contain oats, cubes, flaked maize and bran in balanced proportions, as well as added vitamins and minerals. Some also contain molasses to make them more palatable for finicky feeders. If you choose a well-known brand, you can be sure that your pony is getting a suitable feed.

ROOTS AND APPLES
Root vegetables, such as carrots, swedes, turnips and mangels, are all good for a pony and give variety to his diet. Carrots are particularly popular. Rinse the vegetables first and then cut them into finger-shaped pieces. Avoid round slices as these could stick in a pony's throat and choke him. Apples, both cookers and eaters, should be quartered, core and all. Potatoes are not usually liked by ponies unless they are cooked first. Even then, they may be rejected. Whole turnips and swedes can be left in the field or stable for the pony to nibble at.

SALT
Horses need some salt in their diet, and the easiest way to provide it is to buy a salt block and holder. The holder can be fixed to a fence-post or to the stable wall, so that the pony can lick the block whenever he feels like it. If a grass-kept pony keeps chewing at the

bark of a tree or eating soil, it is a sure sign that he is lacking some essential mineral, most probably salt.

TITBITS

Pieces of apple and carrot make the best titbits as they will not harm the pony's teeth. Nevertheless, most ponies like sweet things, especially sugar lumps, and anything minty is very popular. Beware of giving too many titbits to very small ponies as they come to expect something every time anyone appears, and can be bad-tempered if they are not given a present. It is a sensible practice to give small ponies titbits only in a bucket.

FEEDING TIMES

Try to feed your pony at the same time every day. This is most important in winter when ponies are eager for their food and will come to the regular feeding spot as soon as their internal clock tells them that feeding time is near. If several ponies are waiting to be fed, squabbling and kicking may start if you are late.

When ponies are kept in at night in the winter, it is best to put the feeds ready in the individual loose boxes. Where the stables adjoin the field, all you have to do is to open the gate and the ponies will make for their own boxes of their own accord. You can adjust their rugs, if they wear them, while they are eating, and then leave them to finish their meal in peace.

In summer, your pony may be the only one in the field to have a short feed. In this case, take him out of the field to feed him, if possible out of sight of the other ponies.

CHAPTER 5
Essential equipment

When you first owned a pony, the amount of equipment he needed was fairly small: a snaffle bridle, a general-purpose saddle, a head-collar with lead-rope, tack cleaning and grooming kits are usually all that is needed at that stage. Once you start entering competitions regularly, however, or move on to a livelier second pony, you will begin to build up quite a storehouse of bits and pieces. Not all of them can be classed as essential, but there are a number of items which can help you to put up a better performance.

A SECOND SADDLE

Your general-purpose saddle will be perfectly satisfactory for most of the riding you do. However, there are times when a second, specialist saddle can be quite important.

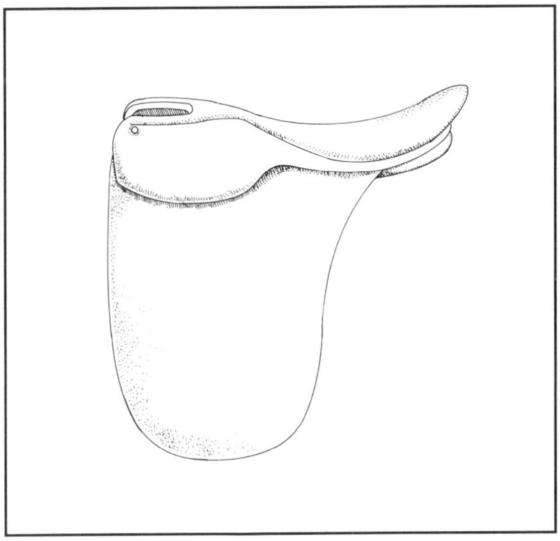

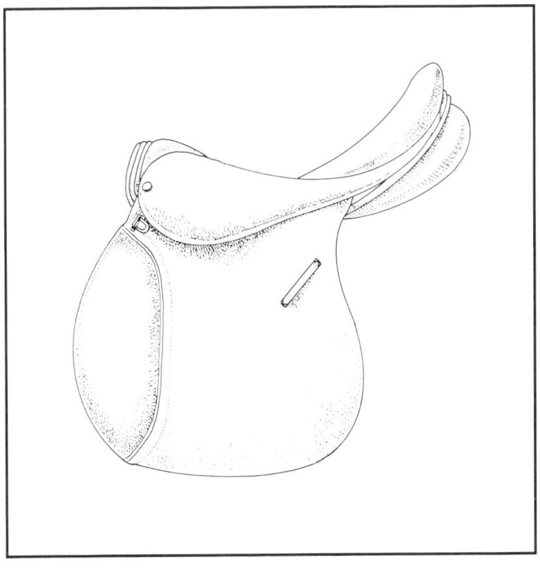

Above Showing saddle, with straight-cut flap.
Left A general-purpose saddle.

Showing saddle A showing saddle is useful if you intend to show your pony in a big way. The flap is straight-cut, which means that there is not much of it in front of your knee. It is designed to show off your pony's shoulders as well as possible and to avoid any interference when he is demonstrating his fine, flowing, extended trot in front of the judges. It goes without saying that you only use this saddle in the show-ring; it is not suitable for general riding.

Dressage saddle A dressage saddle is similar in appearance to the showing saddle, but it usually has a deeper seat and the bars

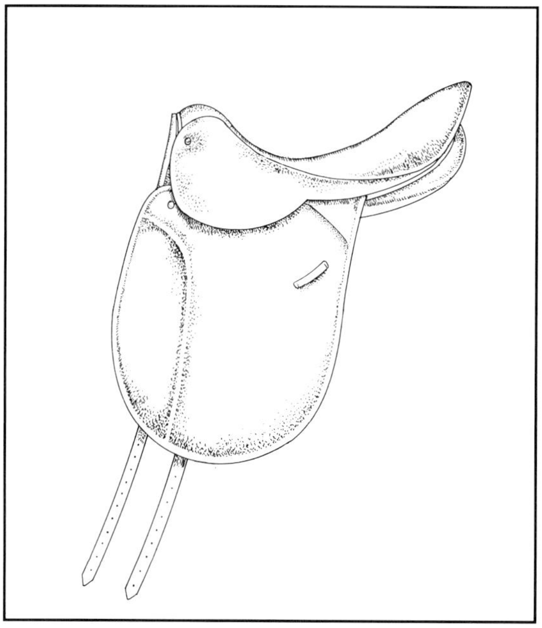

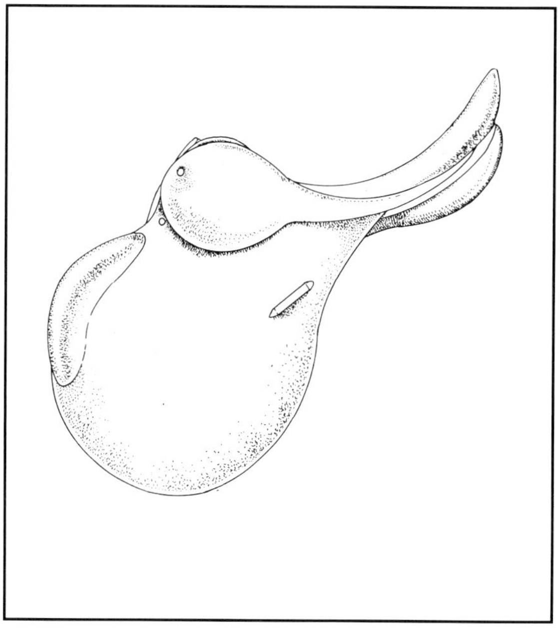

Above left Dressage saddle, with deep seat, short panel and long girth straps.
Above right Jumping saddle, forward cut, with knee rolls.
Opposite A drop noseband, correctly fitted, with the nose-piece high enough not to interfere with the pony's breathing.

are positioned so that each leather hangs down the centre of the flap. The panel is short and the girth straps long. The saddle is designed to place the rider in the dressage position, with the upper thigh almost vertical and the lower leg free. Again, this saddle is intended for the dressage enthusiast, and should not be used for hacking.

Jumping saddle The jumping saddle is very like the general-purpose saddle, except that the flap and panel are more forward-cut and the seat is longer. The effect is to encourage the rider to ride with shorter leathers and to bring her weight over her knees. Very often the forward part of the flap, over the knee rolls, is covered with suede.

If you do acquire a second saddle, for whatever purpose, remember that it should be cleaned regularly to keep it supple and in good condition, even if you use it only on special occasions.

THE BRIDLE

Snaffle bridle For most competitive purposes, a snaffle bridle is best. In Pony Club dressage, a snaffle bit is the only type permitted, and some gymkhana organizers ban the use of curb bits of any description. Nevertheless, there are occasions, for example when out hunting with a strong and lively pony, when you may need more control than a simple jointed snaffle can give you. You can achieve this either by modifying part of the bridle, such as the noseband or the reins, or by switching to a stronger bit.

Double bridle A double bridle is one that has two bits and two pairs of reins. It is used for showing as, in good hands, it reinforces the lessons learned in schooling sessions, resulting in a good natural head carriage and a soft, flexible mouth. A double bridle, however, is not something to be tried out for fun. If you seriously intend to show your pony, you should arrange to have lessons from a competent instructor in the use of a double bridle.

Nosebands

A pony that opens his mouth and crosses his jaw can evade the action of the bit. The answer to this problem is a *drop noseband*, which has a slightly narrower nose-piece than a cavesson does, and is worn below the bit. It is very important to put a drop noseband on correctly because, if the nose-piece is too low, it will interfere with the pony's breathing. The gap between the front of the noseband and the pony's nostrils should be four fingers

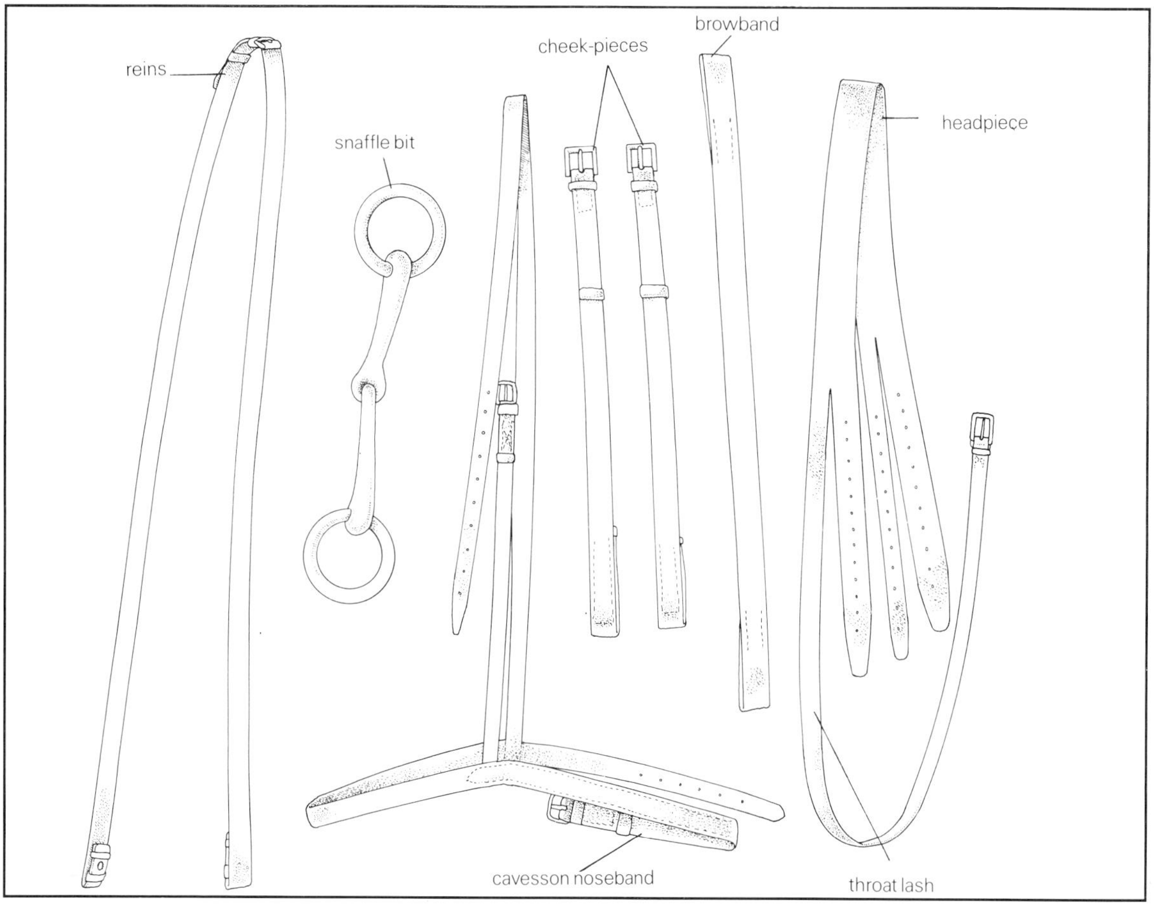

A well-schooled pony should need no more than a plain snaffle bridle; separated into its different parts, **above**, and shown on a pony, **below**.

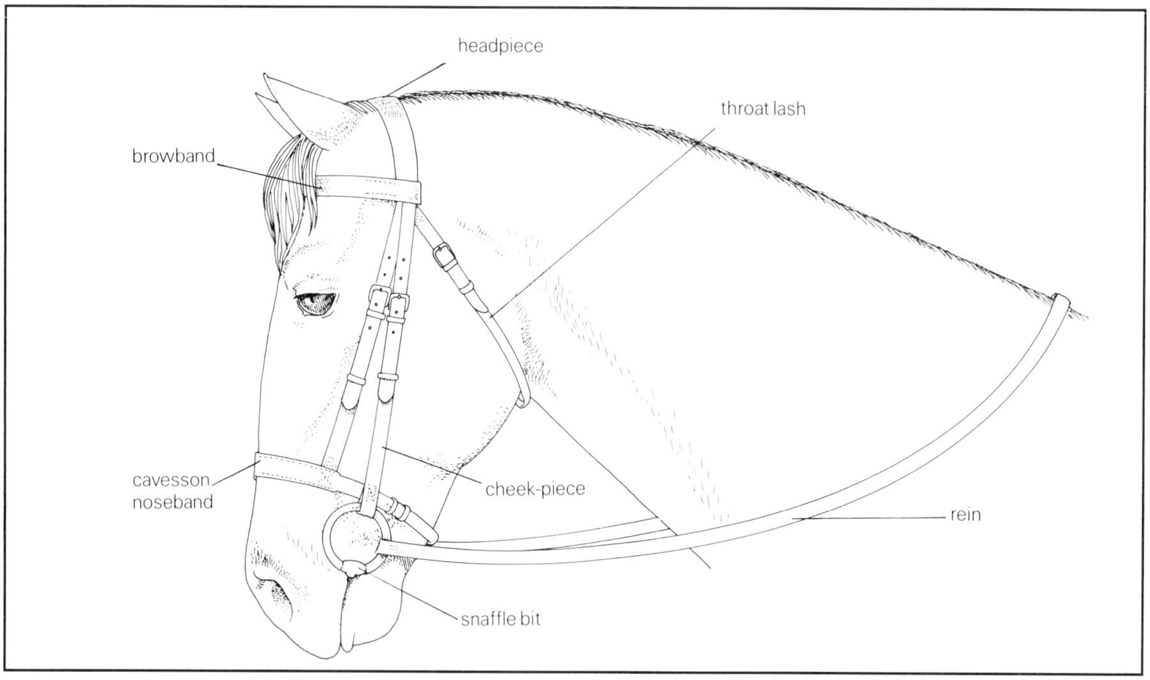

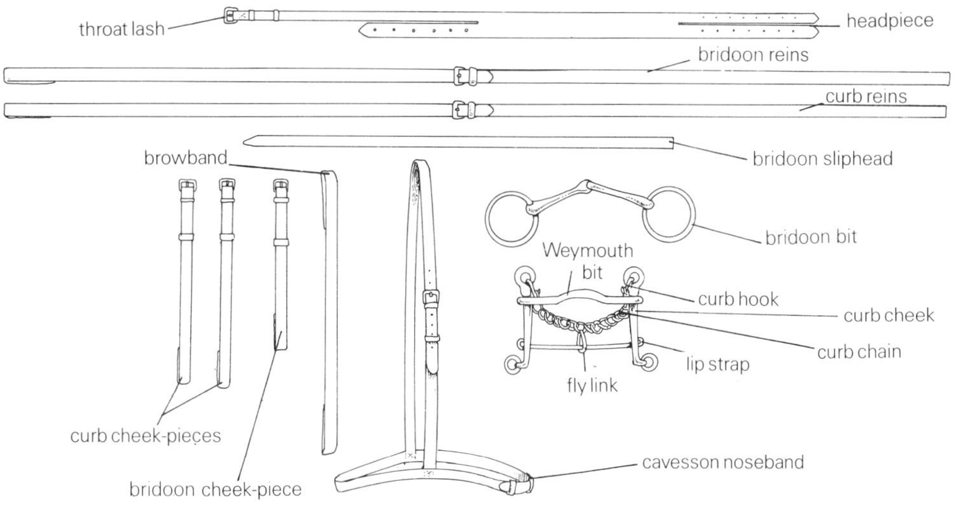

Above The parts of a double bridle.
Below A double bridle in position.

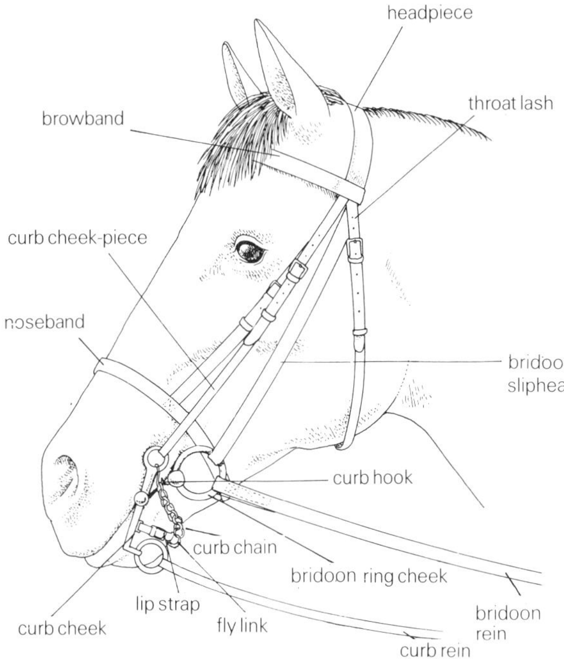

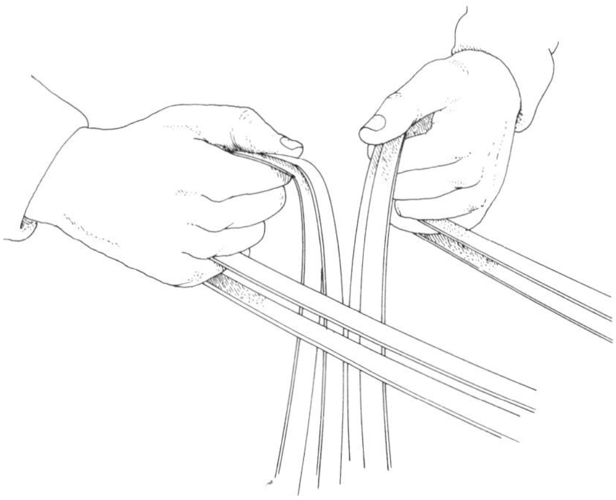

The correct way to hold double reins.

wide with the back resting in the chin groove. It must be tight enough to be effective but not so tight that the pony cannot flex his jaw.

A slightly stronger version of the drop noseband is the *grakle* which has two straps crossing over on the front of the pony's nose and buckled above and below the bit.

If a pony needs both a drop noseband and a standing martingale (see page 38), the *flash* noseband is used. This is a cavesson with a drop noseband attached. The martingale is fixed to the cavesson and not to the drop.

Bits

You should aim to get your pony going well in a snaffle bit. If he resists the bit, this may be due to lack of training – the pony has not yet learned to respond to the signals given to him by his rider; or lack of balance – not unusual in a young pony which is still growing accustomed to the weight of his rider. He may be afraid of the bit, perhaps because it fits badly, or because he has a sore mouth or has had a heavy-handed and unsympathetic rider. In both these cases, it is important for the rider to avoid using force. Patient schooling, under the eye of a competent instructor, should encourage the pony to accept the bit happily, provided that you have made certain that the

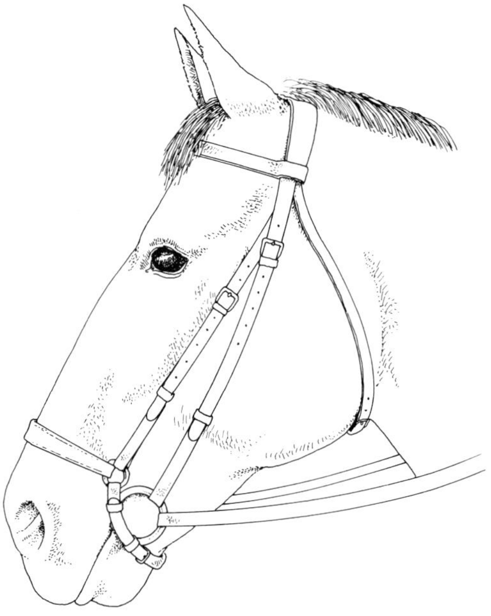

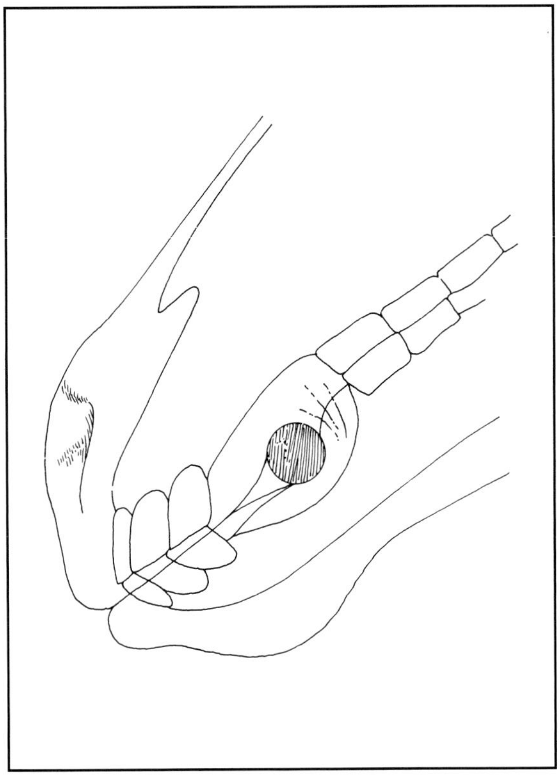

Three nosebands. **Top left** the drop noseband; **top right** the flash; **above** the grakle.

Cross-section of a horse's mouth, showing the gap between the molars and incisor teeth, known as the bars, on which the mouthpiece of the bit bears.

A pony wearing a Pelham bit, fitted with roundings which enable the bit to be used with a single rein.

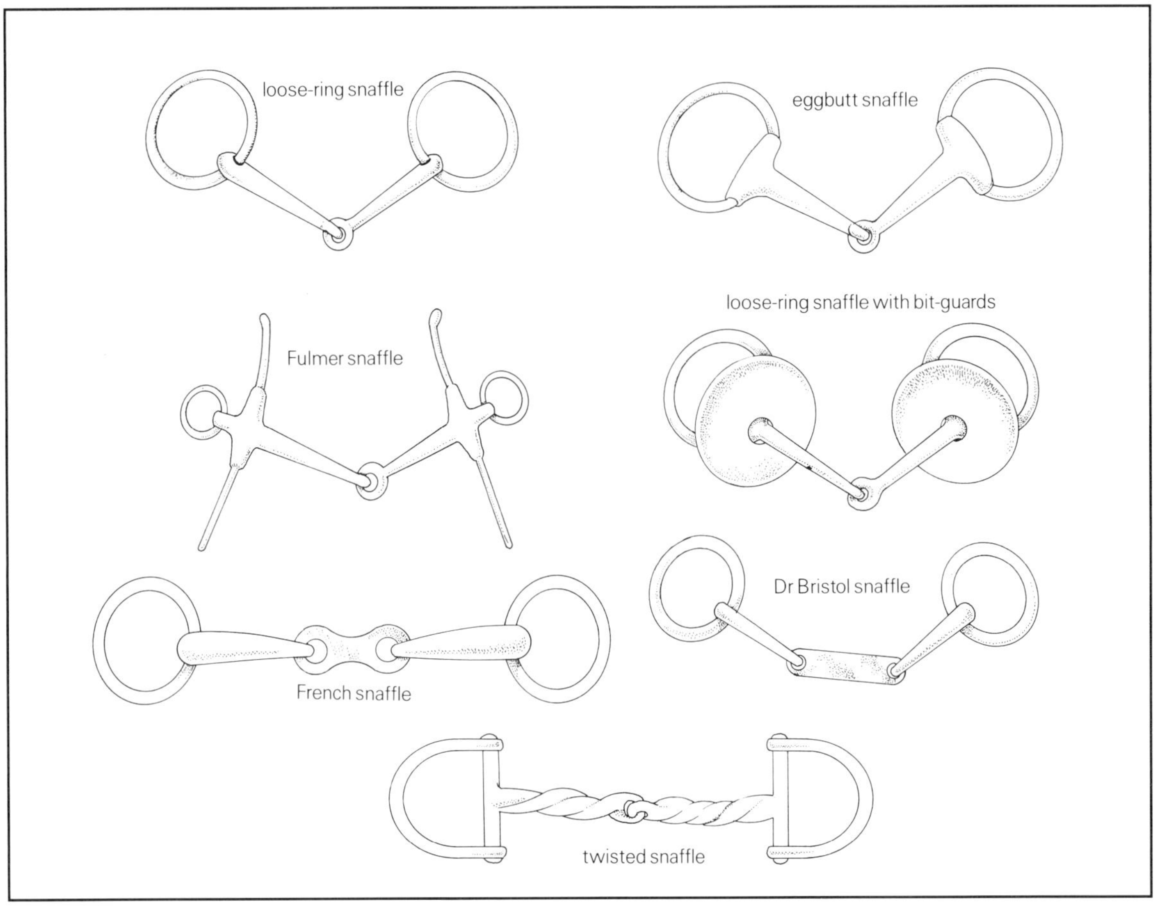

A selection of snaffle bits.

bit is the right size and that he has nothing in his mouth which could be causing him pain.

A bit is the right size if the mouthpiece sticks out on either side about $\frac{1}{2}$cm ($\frac{1}{4}$in) when the joint of the snaffle is straight. It is in the correct position in the pony's mouth if it just wrinkles the corners of the lips.

Snaffle bits Snaffle bits come in various designs. The *loose-ring snaffle* has a jointed mouthpiece, and rings that rotate through the holes at either end of the mouthpiece. It is possible for these rings to pinch, and many people prefer to use the *eggbutt snaffle* which has smooth side joints that cannot pinch. Alternatively, a pair of bit-guards can be used to protect the corners of the pony's mouth from soreness. These are rubber discs that fit over each end of the bit between the mouthpiece and the rings.

A *Fulmer snaffle* has extended cheek-pieces which are attached to the bridle's cheekpieces by leather keepers. These prevent the bit from rubbing the mouth or being pulled from one side to the other.

Snaffle bits with double joints, such as the *French snaffle* and *Dr Bristol*, are useful on ponies with a narrow tongue groove. The French snaffle has a small rounded central plate between the joints and is fairly mild in its action, but the Dr Bristol with an angled rectangular central plate is a severe bit.

The *twisted snaffle* which has a twisted mouthpiece is a severe bit and should not be necessary on a well-trained pony.

Bits for a double bridle The double bridle has two bits, a jointed snaffle called a bridoon, and a *curb bit*, usually a Weymouth, with a curb chain. It is used by experienced riders to give them precise control, and is only used when the pony is well enough trained to respond positively to the lightest aids.

The Pelham bit This bit combines the qualities of a double bridle into a single mouthpiece. The mouthpiece can be straight

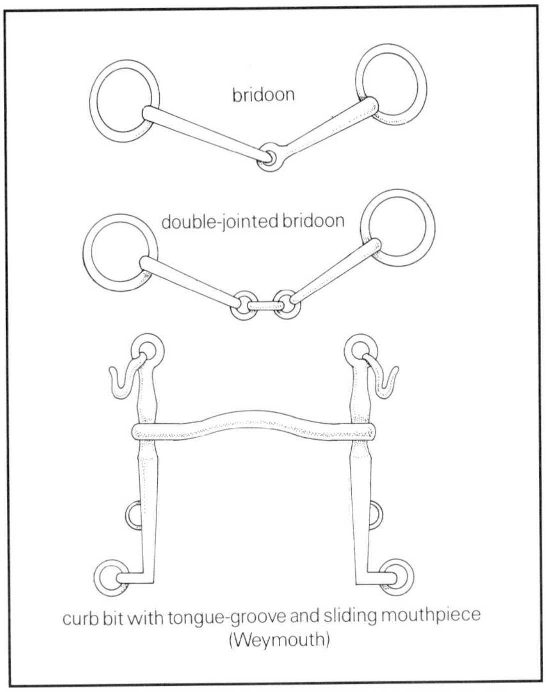

Bits for a double bridle.

Pelham bits.

or curved, and sometimes has a small arch in the centre; the cheek-pieces are fitted with two pairs of rings and a curb chain. When it is tightened, the curb rein, which is attached to the bottom pair of rings, puts pressure on the poll (the top of the pony's head, between the ears) and, through the curb chain, on the chin groove. The top rein acts on the lips, corners of the mouth, tongue and roof of the mouth.

Those who find it difficult to ride with two reins sometimes use a Pelham bit fitted with roundings. These are leather pieces which are attached to the bridoon and curb rings on the bit and enable a single rein to be used.

Although some ponies do seem to go well in a Pelham bit, on the whole it is better to use a snaffle in conjunction with a drop noseband if greater control is needed.

Decoration on bridles

A coloured browband is permissible in all classes except showing events. This is usually made from leather and covered in a shark's tooth pattern of strips of plastic or velvet in contrasting colours. The disadvantage of such a browband is that it is not possible to get at the leather core to oil it and keep it supple. Velvet covered browbands are difficult to clean, but the plastic-covered type just need a wipe over to keep them bright.

Showing browbands may be plain leather or brass-mounted. The brass mounts or studs should be polished. These browbands, however, are not allowed in official Pony Club mounted games competitions.

The noseband may be plain leather or have a stitched pattern on the front part. Both are cleaned in the normal way with saddle soap or leather dressing.

Reins

Narrow reins are often used for showing, but slightly wider reins give a better grip to the hands. Reins of plaited leather, or those covered with rubber, are easier to grip in wet weather. Always measure the reins before buying a new pair, as long reins on a short-necked pony will give too much surplus. The loop will hang so far down that it can catch your foot. Many children, especially when taking part in gymkhana events in which a short rein is necessary, shorten the rein by tying a loose knot in it. Remember to undo the knot before putting the bridle away, or the leather could become damaged or cracked where the knot is tied.

ADDITIONAL TACK

Martingales

Standing martingale One of the commonest problems with a headstrong pony is the habit of throwing up the head in an effort to evade the restrictions imposed by your hands. Once a pony's head gets above a certain point, the action of the bit becomes much less effective, and if your riding is not yet advanced enough to bring his head down through the use of your seat and legs, then some extra control is needed. The use of a standing martingale stops the pony from carrying or tossing his head too high. It consists of a strap with a loop at each end; one end is attached to the underside of a cavesson noseband and the other to the girth. The strap passes between the pony's forelegs, and is supported by a neck-strap.

Standing martingale.

To be sure that a standing martingale is correctly fitted, hold the horse's head in the right position and push the strap upwards with your hand. It should touch the pony's throat. The strap is fitted with buckles to enable adjustments to be made.

Running martingale In this form of martingale, one end is attached to the girth, and it is supported by a neck-strap. The front part of the strap, however, divides into two, and each end finishes in a ring, through which the reins pass. The purpose of this type of martingale is to ensure that pressure via the reins

Running martingale.

on to the bit always comes from the right direction, however much the rider may throw her hands about. To fit the running martingale, attach one end to the girth and check that the rings on the other end reach to the pony's throat. Rubber stops should be attached to the reins to prevent the rings from sliding down and getting hooked over the stud billets or buckles where rein and bit rings meet.

Irish martingale This is a short strap about 10 cm (4 in) long, with a ring at either end, which links the two sides of the pair of reins underneath the pony's neck. Its purpose is to prevent the reins from going over the pony's head.

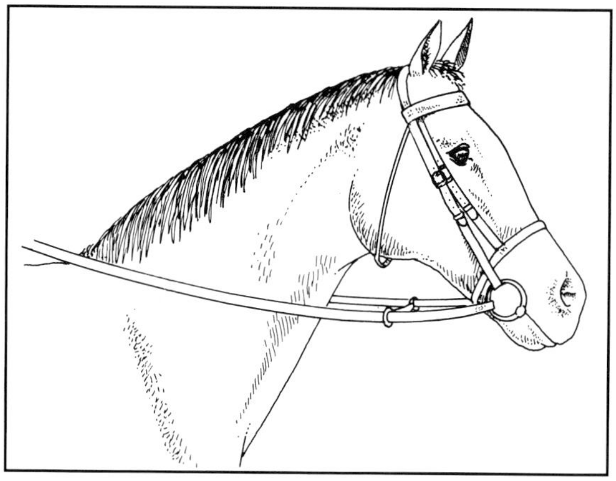

Irish martingale.

Properly fitted running martingale. When the pony's head is in the normal position, as here, the martingale does not interfere with the head carriage. It comes into play only if the pony throws up his head.

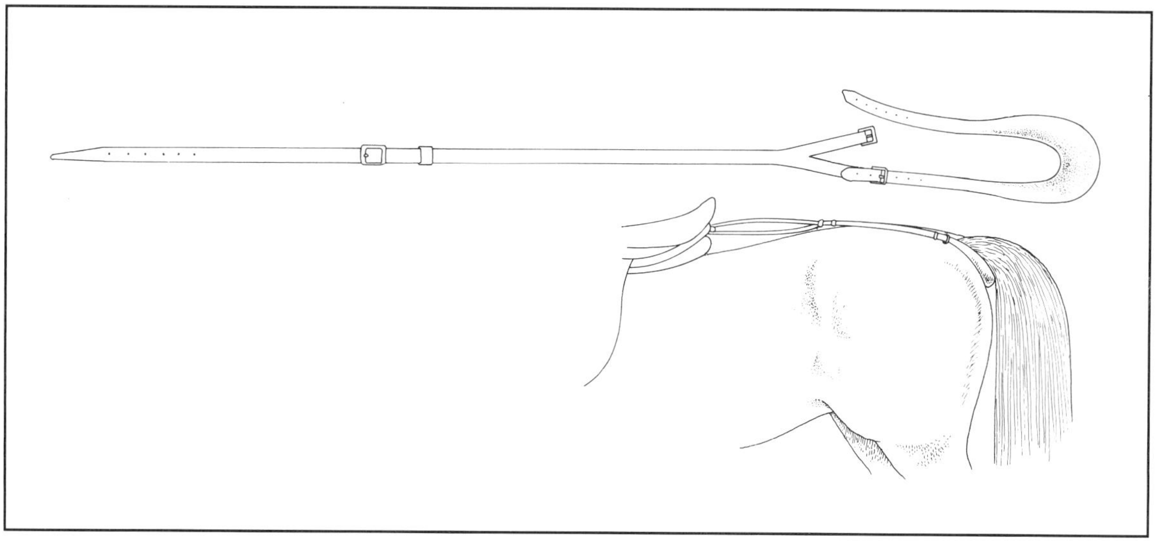

The parts of a crupper, **top**, and in position, **below**.

Breastplate and crupper

Some ponies have flat, low withers, others high, prominent withers: both can make it difficult to keep a saddle in the right place.

If your pony's withers are low, you may find that the saddle tends to slip forwards while you are riding. The remedy could lie in having the saddle re-stuffed and you should consult a reputable saddler on this point. If, however, re-stuffing does not help the answer may be to fit a *crupper*. This is a strap with a padded loop at one end through which the tail passes. The other end fastens to a D-ring on the back of the saddle.

If, on the other hand, the saddle tends to slip back, a *breastplate* will hold it in position. This consists of a neck-strap which is connected to metal D-rings on the front of each side of the saddle by means of two short straps on either side of the pony's neck. A broader strap passing between the pony's forelegs connects the neck-strap to the girth. An alternative to this is the *breast-girth*. This consists of a wide webbing strap which is fastened to the girth straps under the saddle flaps. A short connecting strap over the neck in front of the withers holds the breast-girth horizontally across the pony's chest.

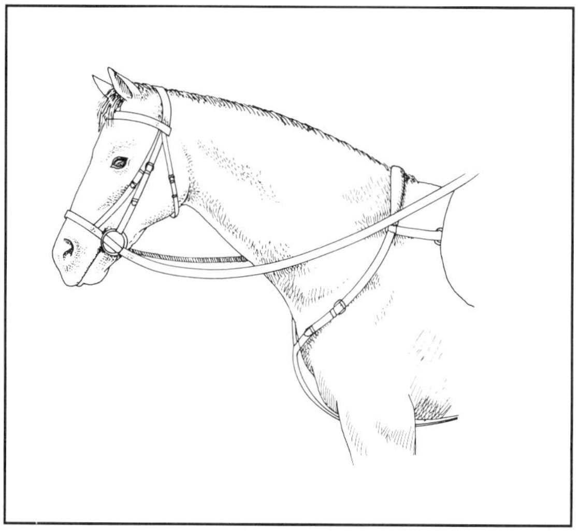

Breastplate.

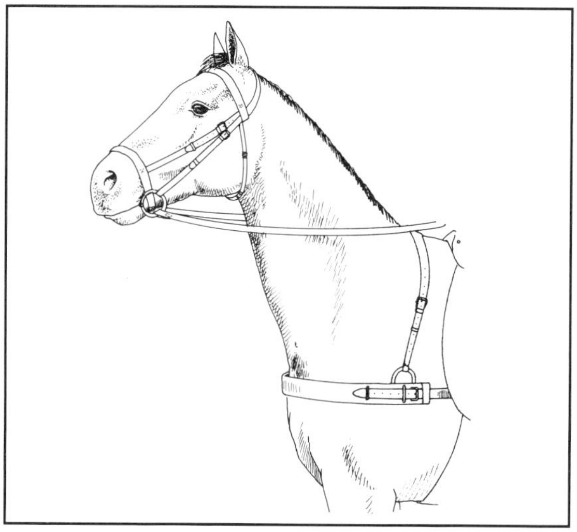

Breast-girth.

Numnah

This is a saddle-shaped pad which is worn under the saddle to protect the back, either when the pony is being ridden for a long period, or as a temporary measure with a saddle that needs re-stuffing. It can be made from a number of different materials, including sheepskin, which is expensive, felt and sorbo-rubber. Some numnahs are quilted. The best sort is made from natural fibres, which are absorbent and do not cause sweating and inflammation. The numnah can be fastened to the saddle by means of straps which pass round the girth straps.

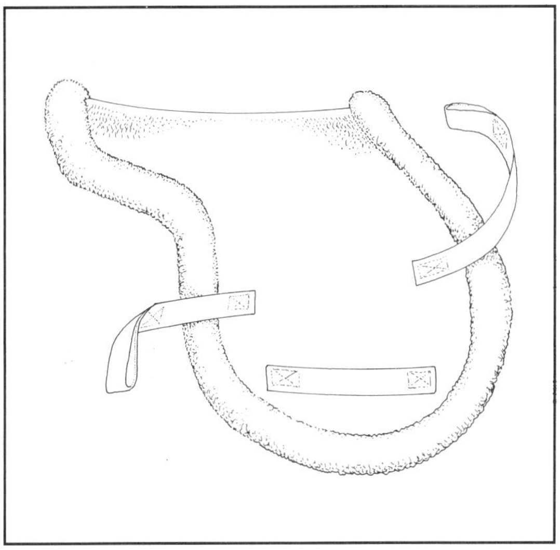

Numnah.

HORSE CLOTHING

Once you start entering competitions regularly and taking your pony to shows in a trailer or horse-box, he will need various forms of protective clothing.

Types of rug

There are many types of rug (called blankets in the USA), each having a different purpose. The decision on which type to buy first can be a difficult one, assuming that you cannot afford to buy three or four at once. And it will be influenced by the time of year when you buy it, as your pony's needs in summer are different from those in the winter. When visiting agricultural or major horse shows, take time to look round the trade stands; it is often possible to pick up a bargain or special show offer, and with so many suppliers gathered together in a small area, you can study and compare prices and quality.

Make certain that you know your pony's measurements. Most rugs are sold in sizes ranging from 1.2 m or 1.3 m to 1.8 m or 2 m (4 ft or 4 ft 6 in to 6 ft or 6 ft 6 in). This measurement represents the length of the pony from a point in the centre of the chest, where the rug's buckles would lie, to a point on the pony's quarters vertically below the root of the tail. Other measurements, such as the depth of the rug and the length along the back, are proportional to the first measurement, so you need only the one measurement to assess the size of rug to buy.

Some rugs are sold with their own surcingle. With others, you have to buy a surcingle or roller separately. Always check whether it is included in the price.

Anti-sweat rugs As a start, an anti-sweat rug is the most useful type. It is made of open cotton mesh and is used on an overheated pony to help him to cool down without catching cold. It can be used on its own or under a second rug, which should be made from natural material. Anti-sweat rugs are usually sold in three sizes: small, medium and large. Because it is rather shapeless, it is better to be too small than too big. It washes easily.

Summer sheets A summer sheet is made of cotton, often in a checked design, and should be supplied with a matching surcingle and fillet-string. It is used to protect a groomed pony from dust and flies, and when travelling in warm weather. The fillet-string is usually a plaited string which is tied to one side of the back edge of the sheet; it passes loosely under the tail and fastens to the other side. Its purpose is to prevent the sheet from blowing in the wind.

Day rugs These are made of wool, usually in a dark colour with a contrasting binding. A day rug will keep a clipped and stabled pony warm when he is standing in his box during the day. The day rug can also be used for travelling.

Night rugs A night rug is worn by a stabled, clipped pony during the night. It is made of jute, often lined with wool. It can, of course, also be used during the day, but, because it tends to get dirty when the pony lies down, it is usually kept for night wear only. It may be supplied with a stitched-on

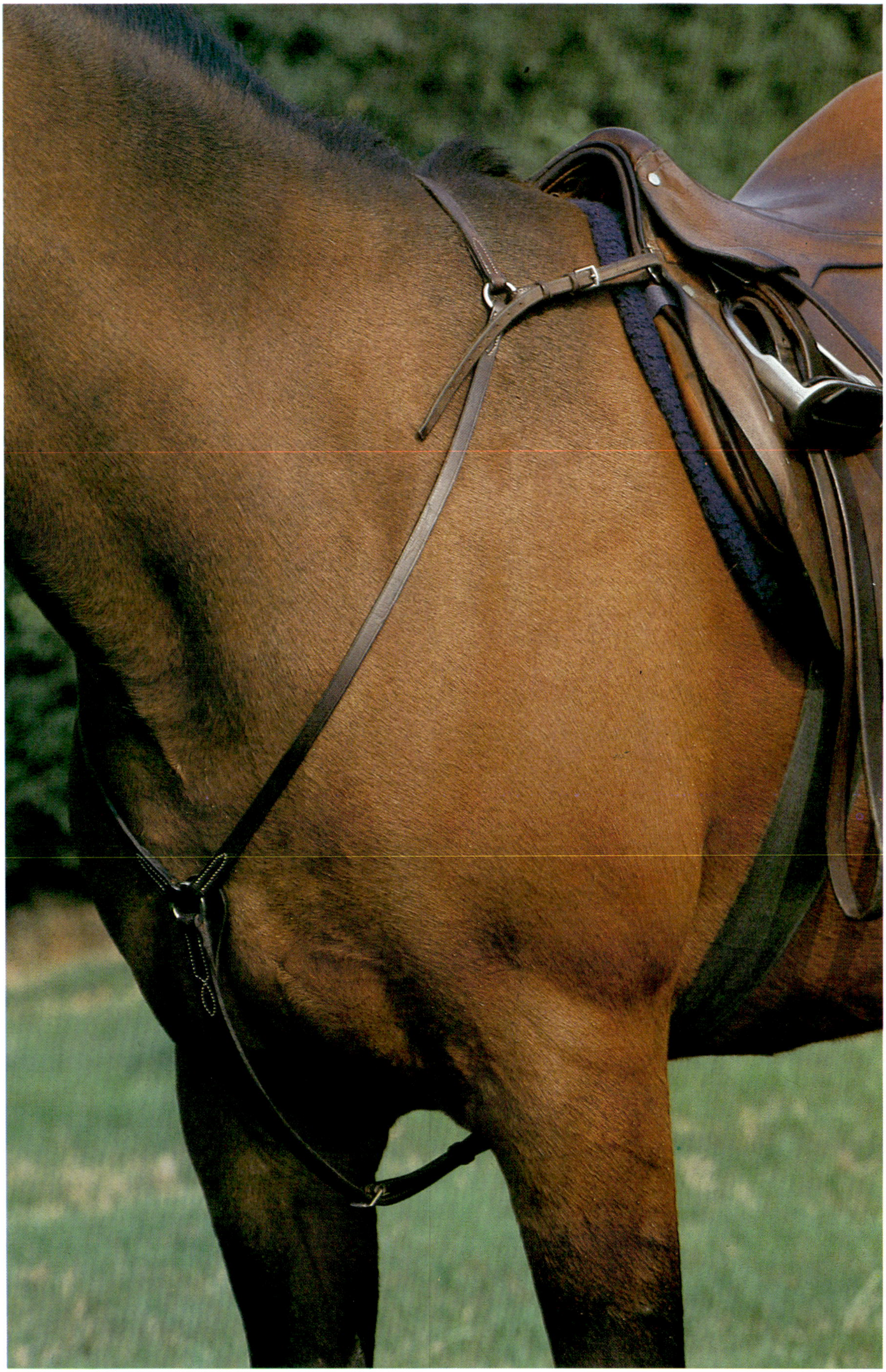

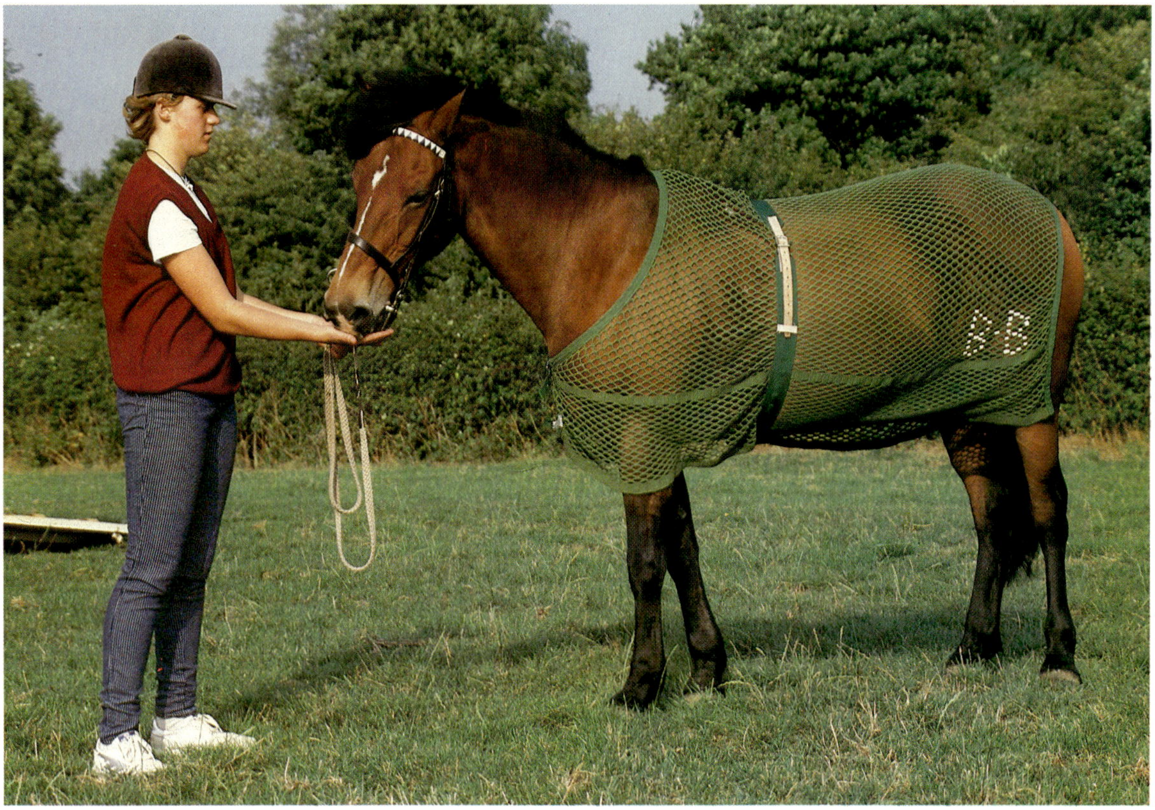

Left A breastplate, used to prevent the saddle from slipping back. **Top** An anti-sweat sheet. The open mesh allows the pony to cool down without getting cold. **Above** The same pony in a summer sheet. This light cotton rug protects the pony from dust and flies.

surcingle, but to avoid unnecessary pressure on the pony's spine the surcingle should be cut off, and a separate roller used instead.

All-purpose rugs These are made of quilted material, usually man-made. An all-purpose rug can be worn by a stabled pony day or night and is easy to keep clean because it can be put in the washing-machine. However, man-made fibres do not breathe, unlike wool or cotton, and can make horses sweat if the weather is mild. It is a very good type of rug for travelling.

In very cold weather, the clipped, stabled pony may need extra warmth during the night. For this purpose, blankets made of wool or acrylic are used and are put on under the night rug.

Exercise rugs This is a short rug, often striped, which covers the horse's loins and quarters when he is being ridden out at exercise. They are mostly used by racehorses. A hardy pony does not usually need an exercise rug even if he is clipped right out and stabled. However, a *waterproof sheet* can be extremely useful, even on a pony normally kept at grass. It protects the pony's back and loins when he is being ridden in very wet weather. The back of the sheet is shaped to fit over the pony's quarters.

New Zealand rugs A New Zealand rug is designed to stay in position on a pony that is loose in a field, even when he rolls. There are, in fact, many different designs, but they all have the same purpose. Some are retained by one or two surcingles or rollers and a system of cross-over straps which pass between the pony's hind legs. Others have diagonal surcingles. Yet others rely on the cut of the rug and judiciously placed tucks to conform to the contours of the pony's body, to prevent it from slipping. A New Zealand rug is unnecessary on an unclipped pony, but they are useful on a clipped pony to replace the protection that his coat would have given him if he had not been clipped.

The disadvantage of a New Zealand rug is that it can chafe, particularly on the points of the shoulder, around the withers and between the hind legs. A pony in a New Zealand rug *must* be caught up and inspected twice daily to make adjustments and reduce the chances of chafing to a minimum.

Rollers and surcingles These are both straps which pass round the pony's belly, just behind the withers, and are fastened by buckles to hold the rug in place. The difference between them is that the roller is fitted on the underside with pads, which rest on either side of the pony's spine and prevent pressure on the spine.

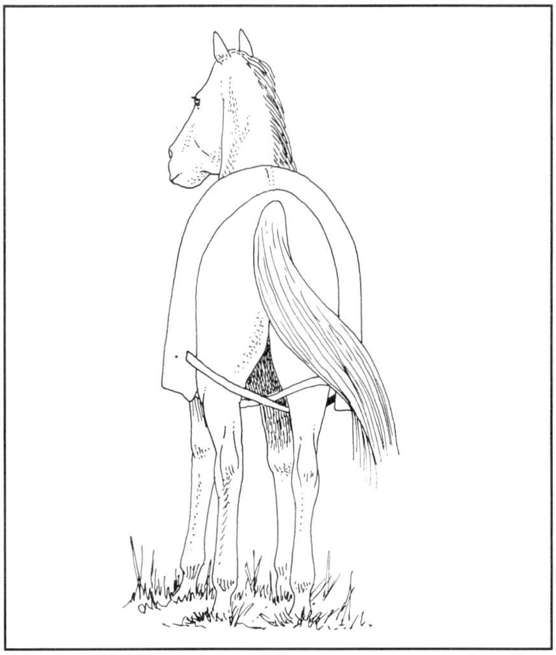

Rear view of New Zealand rug, showing how cross-over leg straps help to keep it in place.

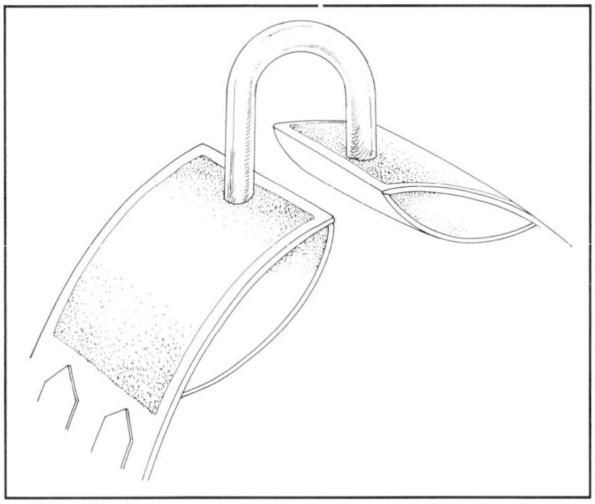

An anti-cast roller.

A *roller pad* is a thick piece of foam rubber which is placed under the surcingle to reduce pressure on the spine. The pad should be wider than the surcingle.

An *anti-cast roller* is made with a projecting bar of metal on the upper part of the roller, above the padded section. It is worn by a stabled horse and stops him from going right over when he rolls, which might cause him to get jammed (cast) against the stable wall. It should not be necessary in a big loose box.

Putting on a rug

Drape the rug over your arm; then with both hands toss it well forward over the pony's withers. Straighten out the front and fasten the chest buckle. Move to the pony's quarters and pull the rug back, again using both hands. As long as your pony does not kick, move behind him and check that the rug is straight and level. Put the roller or surcingle in place, making certain that the end with the buckle passes under the belly. Place the roller pad in position and do up the roller. It should be firm but not too tight. Remove wrinkles in the rug by running your fingers between roller and rug on both sides. Make certain that there is no drag on the shoulders. The roller should lie in the same place as the girth on a saddle, just behind the elbow.

If a blanket is being used, this goes under the rug and should be adjusted to ensure that the back end of the blanket is level with the edge of the rug. Any surplus blanket at the neck end is folded back after the roller or surcingle has been fastened.

Removing a rug

Undo and remove the roller or surcingle. Undo the chest buckle. Fold the front part of the rug over the back. Grip the centre front with your left hand and the centre back with your right and sweep the rug off over the quarters in one movement. When a blanket has been used, both blanket and rug are taken off at the same time. Shake the rug and blanket outside, fold up and place them in a safe dry place, clear of the ground. Always keep a rug and its surcingle together.

Protection while travelling

Although partitions in a trailer or horse-box may be padded, and the floor covered with a thick bed of straw or shavings, a pony can easily bang himself if he is caught off-balance by the vehicle's movements. To minimize the risk of injury, it is sensible to give him as much protection as possible.

Many ponies, even those which are good travellers, sweat with anticipation or excitement when they are in the confines of a trailer. To be sure that he arrives in good

The position of a blanket when worn under a rug. **Left** The blanket is put on first, well forward up the neck, and the front corners are folded up so that they lie on the neck. **Right** The rug is put on over the blanket, and the corners of the blanket are folded back and secured under the roller.

BIANCA

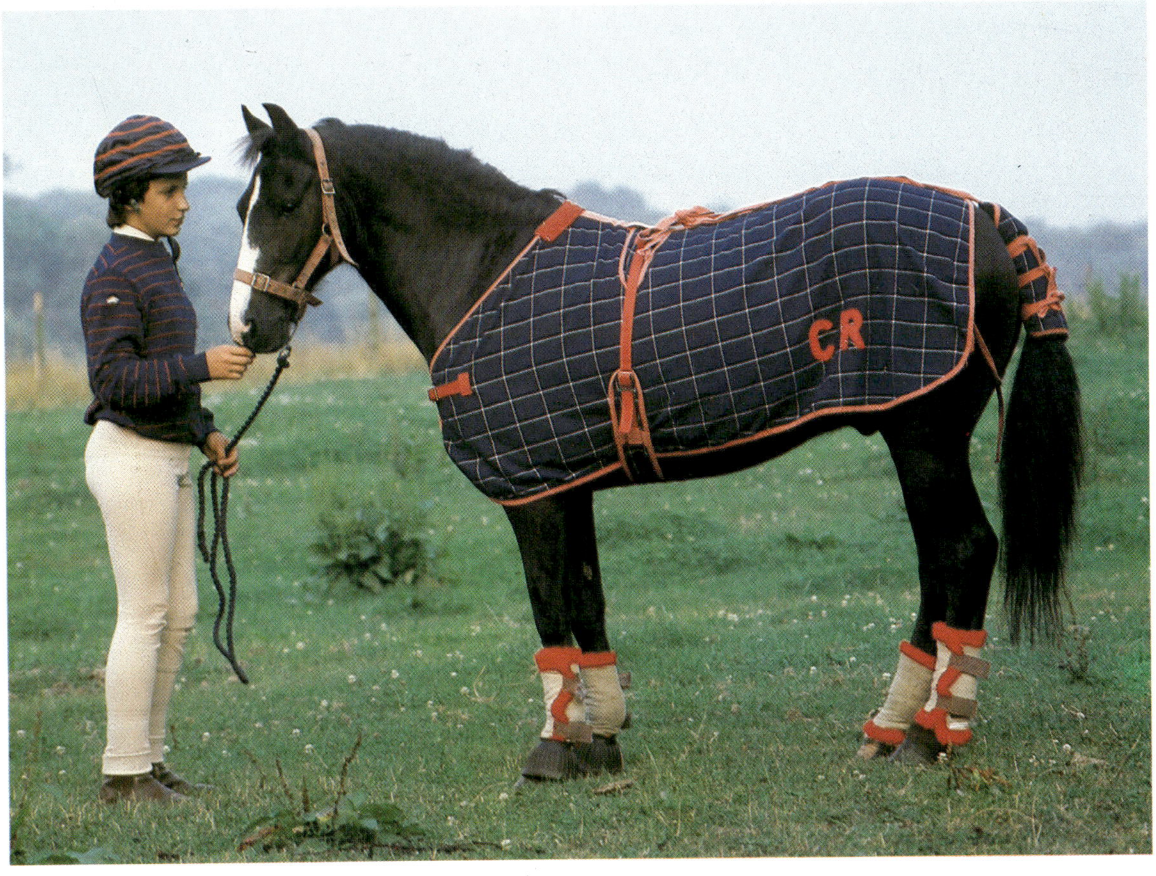
CR

condition, put him in an anti-sweat rug, with or without a sheet or day rug on top. The front of the day rug can be folded back and tucked flat under the roller or surcingle. A pony should never travel in a rug without a roller to keep it in place, as the rug might slip off during the journey and cause the pony to panic.

Stable bandages or *travelling boots* will protect the pony's legs. Travelling boots are made from fleece-lined rectangular pieces of leather, plastic or canvas. They fasten round the leg and come well down over the coronet. They are held in place by straps with Velcro fastenings, and are quick and easy to put on and remove.

Knee caps and *hock boots* may be used if necessary to guard against injury to the leg joints. A *poll pad* will protect the top of the pony's head if he is nervy and therefore likely to throw up his head when he is moving into or out of a trailer.

A *tail bandage* is needed to protect the tail if it gets rubbed against the closed-up trailer ramp. It can be covered in addition by a *tail guard*: a wedge-shaped piece of material that fastens with tapes round the tail, and is attached by tapes at the pointed end to the surcingle.

Bandages

Stable bandages These are designed to keep legs warm, and to help legs which have become wet during a ride to dry off, therefore reducing the risk of chapping. They are made of wool or stockinette and are usually available in sets of four. They should be put on tight enough to stop them from slipping but

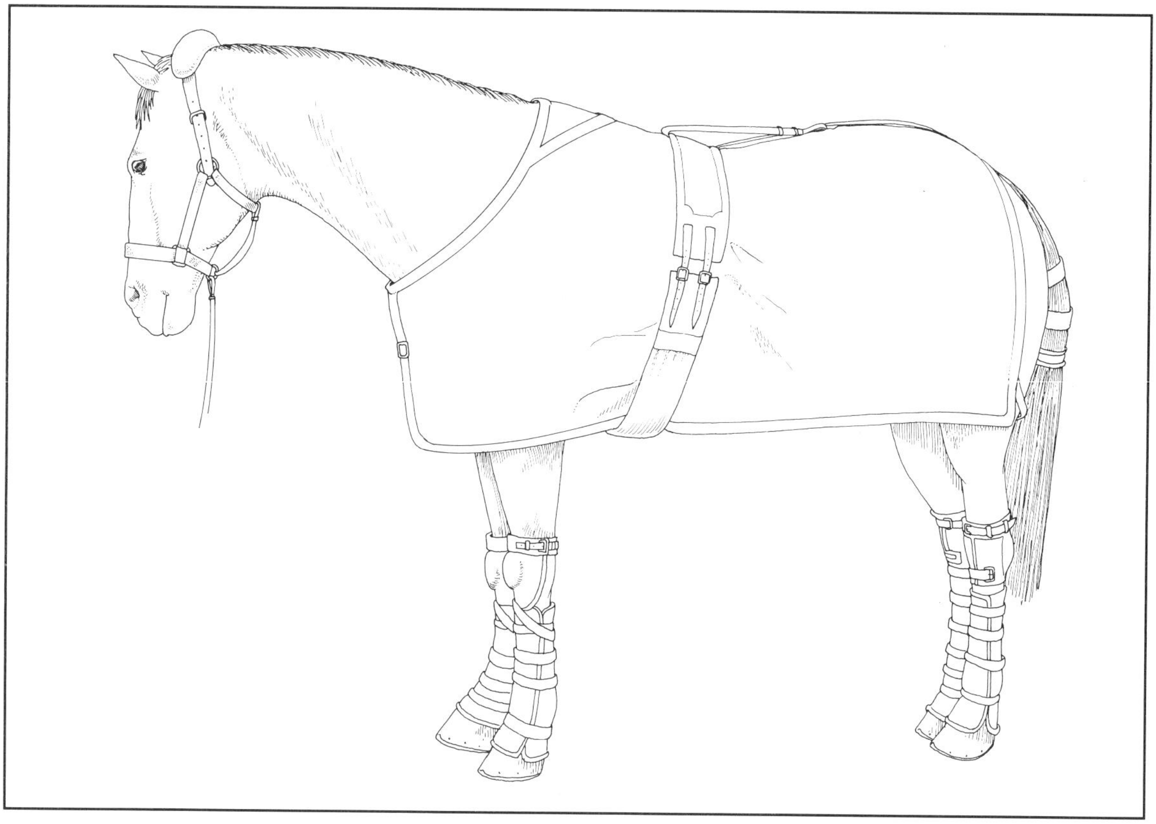

Above Ready for travelling. The pony wears a day rug, with surcingle and fillet string, poll guard, tail guard, knee caps, hock boots and travelling boots.
Pages 46–7 Top left Day rug made of wool and bound with a contrasting colour. **Bottom left** Quilted all-purpose rug with its own attached surcingle. This type of rug, which washes easily, may be used for night or day wear. **Top right** New Zealand rug of the right size for this pony. It protects the back and loins but is not too long to interfere with the pony's movements. **Bottom right** Ready for travelling. The pony wears a summer sheet, fleecy leg guards which reach to the coronet and a tail guard over his tail bandage.

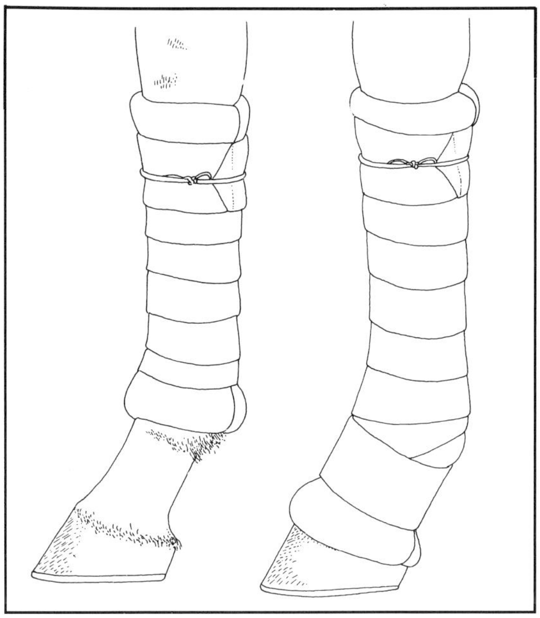

Bandages in position. **Left** Exercise bandage; **right** stable bandage.

not so tight that they cause marks or lumps on the leg. If *gamgee* is used underneath the bandages, this will help to prevent damage to the legs.

A leg should be bandaged downwards from just below the knee. Stable bandages cover the fetlock and reach to the coronet. Start by holding the free end of the bandage against the leg and take a turn round the leg to hold the end in place, fold the free end down, secure it with the next turn of the bandage, and continue down the leg to the coronet. Now bandage upwards until you are back where you started, by which time you should have come to the end of the bandage. Fasten off, either by tying the tapes in a bow or using the clips or Velcro provided. The knot should lie on the outside of the leg, but not on the front or back where it could press on the bone or tendon.

Exercise bandages These are made of an elasticated material, and are designed to give support to the legs while the pony is working. For this reason an exercise bandage stretches from just below the knee to just above the fetlock joint. Gamgee, cotton wool or foam rubber should be wrapped round the leg, and should be completely flat; the bandage is put on over it. Gamgee that protrudes at either end can be trimmed with scissors. The exercise bandage is put on in the same way as the stable bandage except that the upward bandaging begins just above the fetlock joint. Fasten the tapes on the outside of the leg, and for extra security, wrap a band of insulating tape round the leg, over the knot.

Protective boots

Injuries to legs can be caused by bad conformation, poor shoeing, bad riding, inexperience (especially in a young horse), tiredness or an accident. The latter two most commonly occur in competitive riding, especially cross-country. The former can, hopefully, be prevented by good schooling, careful choice of farrier, or the genuine desire on the part of the rider to improve.

In all cases, however, some protection can be given to the pony by using one or other of the various types of protective boots available.

Overreach boots These are bell-shaped and made of rubber. They fit round the lower part of the pastern to protect the heels of the front feet, especially the bulbs of the heels, from damage caused by overreaching. It is caused by the toe of the rear foot striking or

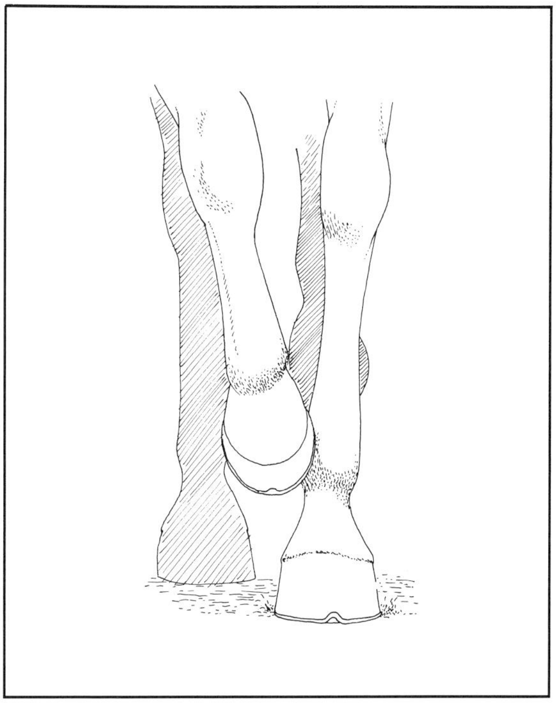

Brushing. The inside of one hoof is interfering with the opposite leg, which can cause injury. Brushing boots will prevent the pony injuring himself by this habit.

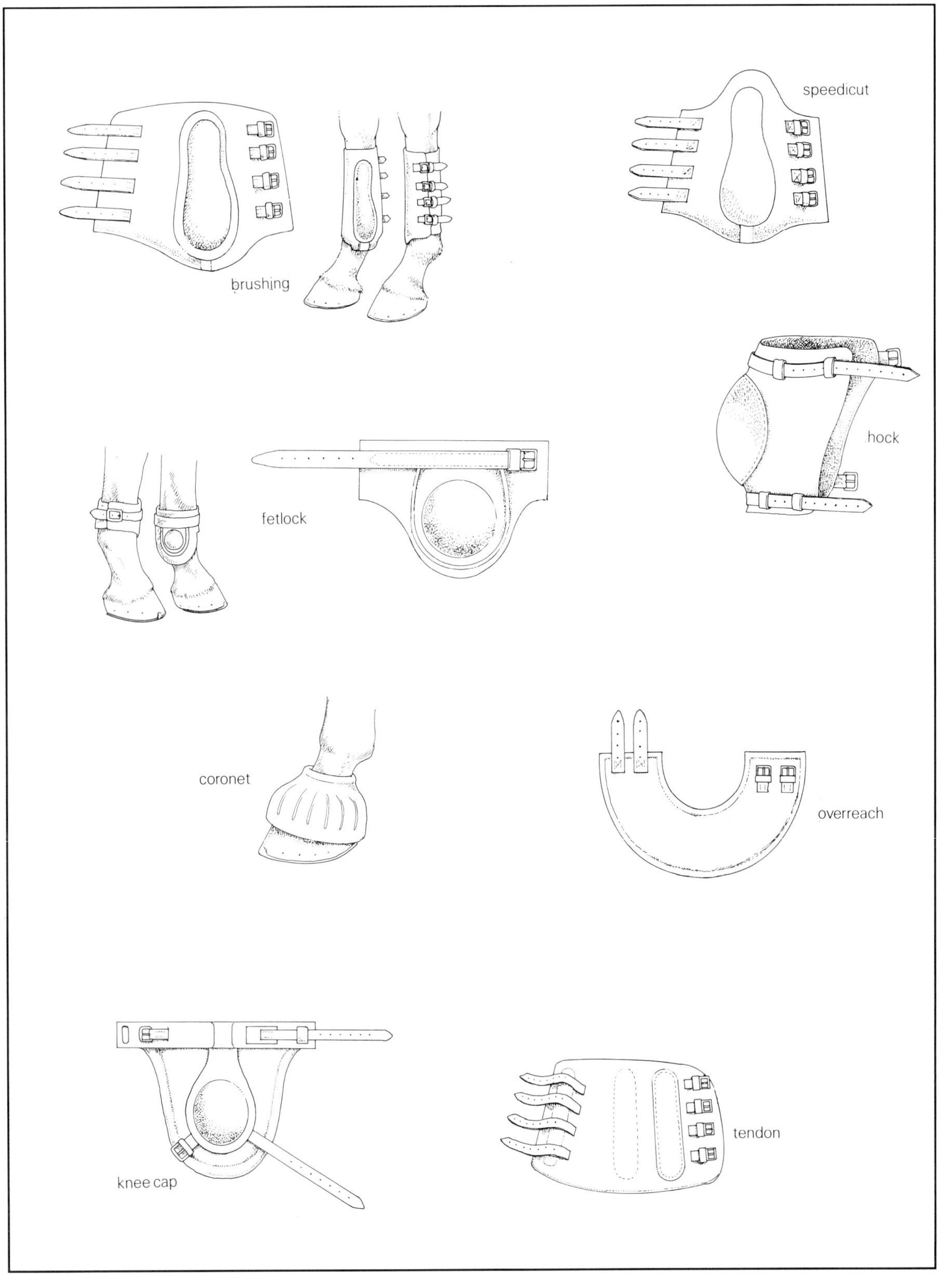

Protective boots.

treading on the heel of the front. It is usually an accidental injury, which can happen while galloping or jumping, particularly in soft ground.

Brushing boots These protect the inside of the leg from injury caused by a blow from the opposite foot. Careful shoeing may help to prevent brushing if it is caused by bad conformation. Made of felt and leather, they have extra padding on the part which covers the inside of the leg, and are fastened on the outside by four or five straps or Velcro fasteners. Ordinary brushing boots protect the fetlock joint and the part of the leg above it almost as far as the knee. *Fetlock boots, Yorkshire boots* and *rubber rings* protect only the fetlock joint.

Speedicut boots These are similar to brushing boots but are worn higher up the leg and protect the inside of the knee joint from injury by the opposite foot. Speedicutting is more dangerous and the wounds usually more severe than those caused by brushing.

Coronet boots These protect the coronet region from being trodden on by other ponies. For this reason they are often used on horses travelling in company.

Tendon boots These have padding at the rear of the leg and protect the tendons from a high overreach.

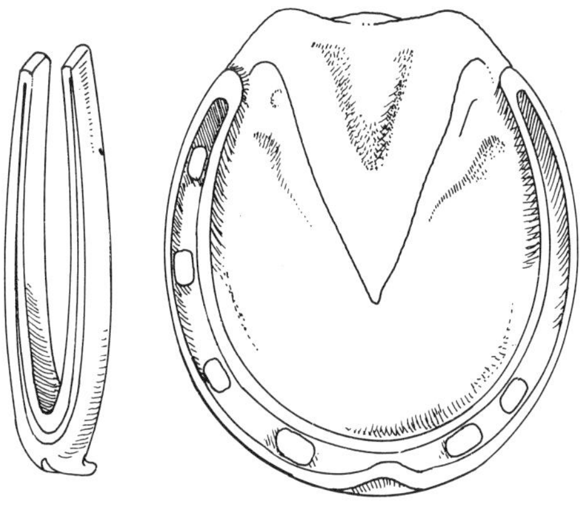

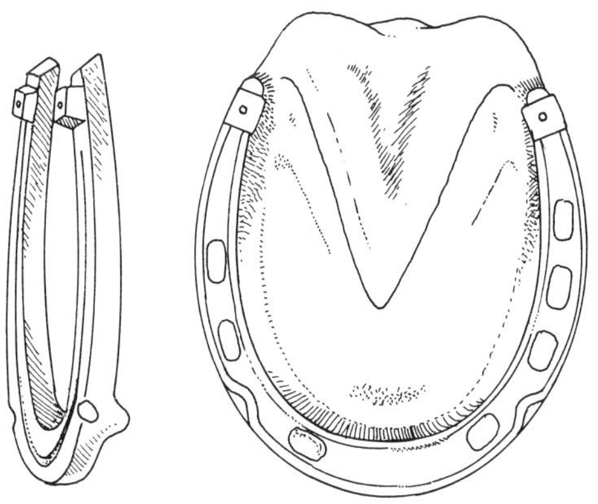

Left: A front shoe with a feathered edge. This shoe will help to correct faults, such as brushing, that are due to weak conformation.
Right: Hind shoe fitted with studs. Studs are used to give a pony better grip when he is jumping or competing in gymkhanas on slippery ground.

CHAPTER 6

Shows and competitive events

PREPARATION

At any show, your pony should look as smart as possible – and so should you. If you arrive at a show with the pair of you scruffy and ungroomed, you will soon get a reputation as someone who does not look after her pony properly, even if this is not true. If you cannot be bothered to remove dirt and sweat marks from your pony or to brush the tangles out of his mane and tail, he will feel uncomfortable and will certainly not give of his best. You might catch the judge's eye, but not in a complimentary way.

Preparation for shows can be divided into two types: that which is carried out at the beginning of the season, such as mane-pulling, clipping and trimming; and that which is done early on the day itself or on the evening before.

Mane- and tail-pulling

The purpose of pulling hairs from the mane and tail is to give them a tidy appearance.

The mane In the case of the mane, pulling will encourage an untidy mane to lie flat, it will reduce a very long mane to a neater length, and will thin out an over-thick mane, making it easier to plait. You should always start with the underside of the mane, removing a few long hairs at a time, by wrapping them around your fingers or around a mane comb and pulling them out quickly with a swift tug. Always do this when the pony is warm, such as just after exercise, as the pores of the skin will be open and the hairs will come out more easily. Never pull hairs from the top of the mane, and take care not to end up with several short hairs which will stick up when the mane is plaited.

The tail The tail is pulled around the dock area and makes the top of the tail look neat and tidy. It saves the bother of plaiting it for showing classes. The tail on a pony kept at grass, however, should *never* be pulled, as he

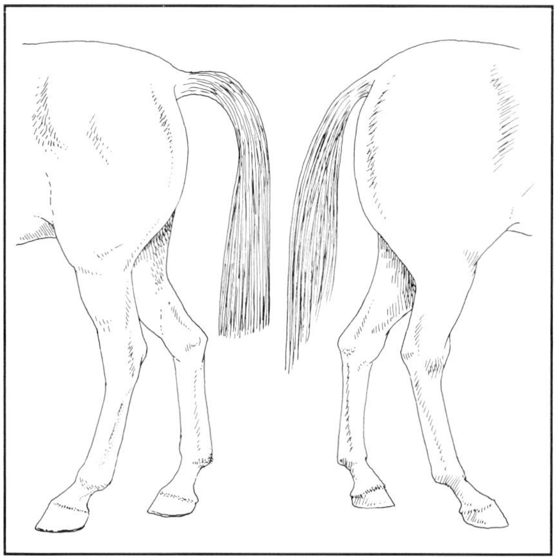

Left A bang tail, unpulled. **Right** A switch tail.

needs the bushy hairs around the top of the tail for protection against the weather.

To pull a tail, first brush it thoroughly to remove any tangles. Then dampen the top of the tail with a water brush. Pull hairs from the underneath part first, then gradually work downwards and sideways, removing hair evenly from both sides of the tail. Stop pulling when you reach a point about half-way down the tail bone.

To finish off, ask someone to hold the tail in a natural position by putting her arm under the root of the tail and lifting it. Using scissors, cut off the ends square at a point just below the hocks. This is known as a *bang tail.* Alternatively, you can continue pulling the tail much further down, leaving the ends of the tail hairs growing to a natural point. This is a *switch tail.*

When pulling is finished, use a tail bandage to preserve the shape.

Tail-pulling is the only occasion when a mane comb can be used on the tail, and then only to help with the pulling. A mane comb used on the tail can break or split the hairs. Clippers and scissors should never be used on either a mane or tail, except to trim the end of the tail (using scissors), or to cut short a small section of mane in front of the withers, and on the poll where the headpiece of the bridle rests.

Other trimming

Scissors or clippers may be used in summer to tidy up the fetlock regions and to remove unnecessary feather. In winter, however, a grass-kept pony must be allowed to keep his fetlocks well feathered as the hair there helps to protect his heels. Overlong whiskers around the muzzle may also be trimmed in summer.

Clipping

Clipping is the removal of all or part of the pony's coat in order to stop him from sweating too much during heavy work; to enable him to do the work without getting too hot and to dry off quickly afterwards; and to make grooming easier.

Full clip All the coat is removed, including the head and legs. It should only be used on a pony which lives in throughout the winter.

A hunter clip.

1

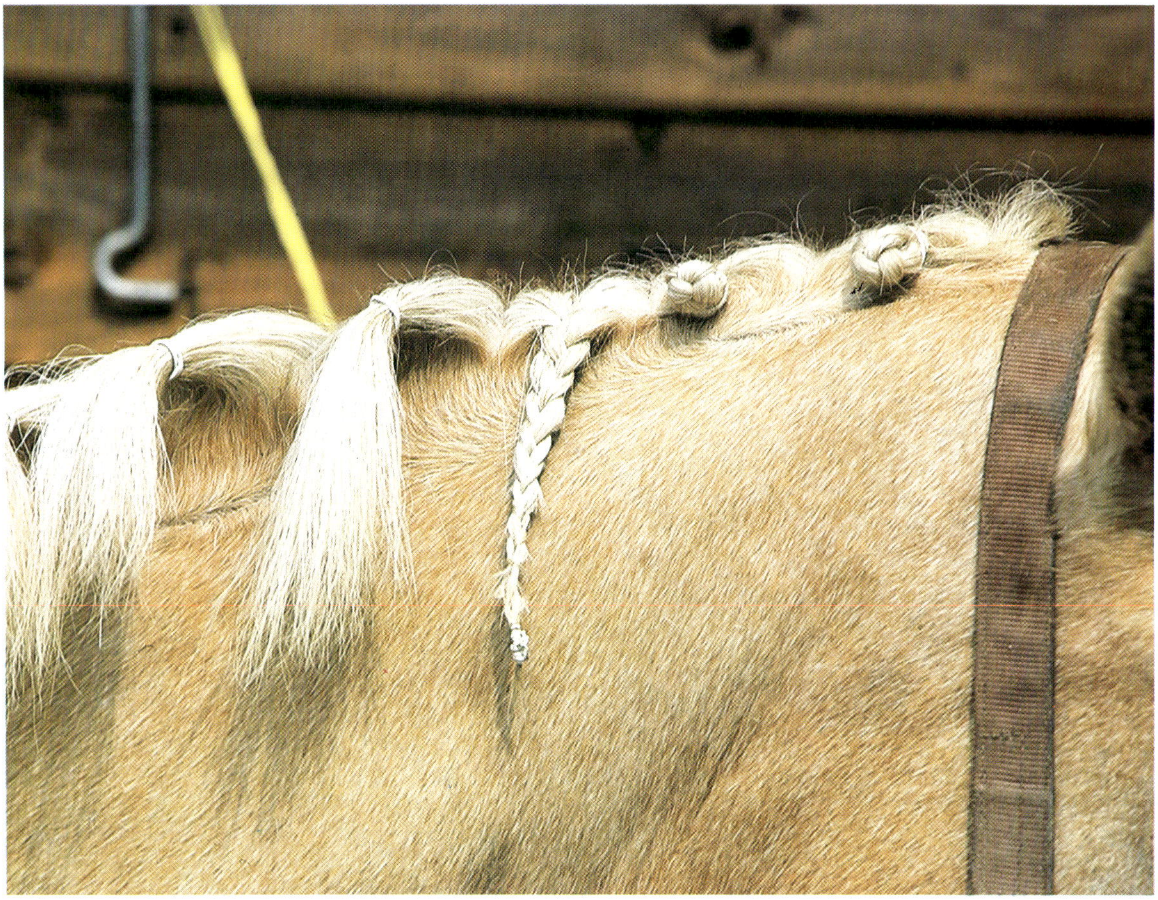

2

3

4

5

Top Blanket clip **Above** Trace high clip.
Pages 54–5 Getting ready for a show. Mane plaiting. **1** Always start at the head-end and divide the hair into the appropriate number of plaits with rubber bands. **2** Try to make the plaits the same size and evenly spaced. **3** The finished plaits make the pony look smart and help to show off his neck and head. Tail-plaiting. **4** The plait should lie centrally down the tail and the hairs drawn in from either side should be regular in size and spacing. **5** Finish off by making one long plait down the full length of the tail before bending it up to form a loop.

The belly clip, is a useful clip for a pony wintering out.

Hunter clip All the coat is removed except for a patch on the back in the shape of a saddle and on the legs as far up as the elbows and thighs. The reason for leaving some of the coat on is to give the pony protection from cold, mud, thorns and cracked heels while hunting, and to prevent the saddle from causing a sore back. A pony with this sort of clip can be turned out into a field during the day in winter, provided he is given a well-fitting New Zealand rug, but he must be brought into a stable at night.

Blanket clip An area of the coat in the shape of a blanket is left on the body and on the legs. It is often used on ponies which are stabled at night but live in a field during the day. The pony will need a New Zealand rug when he is in the field.

Trace-high clip The hair is removed only from the belly and underside of the neck, and on the outside of the flanks and front legs in a position corresponding to where the traces would go on a harness horse. It is a popular clip for ponies kept permanently at grass. Ponies with this clip would usually wear a New Zealand rug.

Belly clip This is an excellent clip for ponies living out all the time. The coat is removed under the belly, between the forelegs and in a narrow strip up the lower part of the neck. A pony with this clip will not get too hot while out hunting or on a strenuous ride. He would not need a New Zealand rug since the rug would not cover the clipped areas anyway.

If you want to have your pony clipped, you should ask an experienced person to do it. Clipping requires some skill as the machine head must not be allowed to overheat (most people nowadays use electric clippers). The machine needs to be well oiled, so that it is not too noisy, and the blades should be sharp. Obviously, there has to be a first time for everyone, but if you wish to do your own clipping, you should carry it out under supervision, however calm your pony may be.

Turn-out for competitions

In some competitions a plaited mane is obligatory. In any showing class, except in-hand and ridden classes for registered native ponies, where a flowing mane and tail are characteristics of the breed, you would be expected to present your pony with the mane and tail plaited up. The original reason for plaiting was to display the pony's neckline to

21

C. RUSSELL

the best advantage, and it has now become part of turn-out requirements. Showing classes include working hunter pony events, where, although the showing is secondary to the jumping, display and turn-out are still important. You should plait for any dressage competition, including the dressage phase of a one-day event. You should also plait when going hunting. You need not plait, however, for show-jumping and cross-country, although many people do.

Plaiting

The mane A really neat row of plaits, of matching size and evenly spaced, can be achieved only by practice, so never be depressed at your first efforts. You can only improve. It does not matter how many plaits you have as long as there is an odd number along the neck, plus one for the forelock. For the best results, do not shampoo your pony's mane just before you intend to plait. Like human hair, a clean, shampooed mane becomes slippery and fly-away and is almost impossible to plait neatly. It is easier to make tight little plaits if the hair of the mane is slightly greasy.

The quick and easy way is to use rubber bands on each plait. Dampen the mane with a water brush, and divide it into the number of plaits you intend to do. Plait each section in turn, winding a rubber band several times round the end of each plait. Your pony now has a row of little pigtails along his neck. Each pigtail must now be rolled up into a tight ball and secured with another band. The plaits should always be rolled under and fit snugly against the crest.

When rubber bands are used alone, the plaits are easier to undo at the end of the day. They can work loose and one or two may come undone completely, but this method is by far the quickest if you are in a hurry.

For more secure and, on the whole, neater plaits, sewing is the best method. Even when sewing, many people use rubber bands to secure the ends of the pigtails, turning to needle and thread to keep the plaits tight when they are rolled up. You will need a reel of button thread in a colour that matches your pony's mane, and a needle with a large eye. After completing the pigtails, cut off a length of thread and pass it through the needle. Take a few turns of the thread round the end of the plait, fold it under once and push the needle through the plait about half-way up. Fold the plait under once more and push the needle through again. Wind the thread tightly round the plait, secure the ends and cut off the thread close to the plait.

Plaiting is best done on the morning of the show, but it is a lengthy business and if you are worried about time you can plait the night before. Never, however, plait the night before if your pony is in the field overnight. He will almost certainly rub the plaits which could damage the mane or, at best, you will have to do them all over again in the morning.

With a stabled pony, some people plait to the pigtail stage the previous evening and tackle the sewing stage in the morning. Alternatively, a good way of preserving the plaits overnight is to cover the whole row of plaits with an old nylon stocking, using a rubber band to hold it in place over each plait.

The tail Tail plaiting is an excellent way of making the top of the tail look neat without depriving a grass-kept pony of the protection a full tail provides. To plait the tail, start at the top, taking in a few hairs from either side in turn, until the plait reaches about two-thirds of the length of the dock. Continue plaiting downwards, using only the centre hairs, until you have a long pigtail hanging the full length of the tail. Secure the end tightly with thread. Fold the end under to form a loop and stitch it to the plait at the point where you stopped taking in side hairs.

Pages 58-9 Correct wear for pony and rider for different types of competition. Page 58: **Top** For show-jumping tweed hacking jackets are usually worn. **Bottom left** A plain coloured jacket for a showing class. **Bottom right** A tweed jacket for Pony Club dressage. Page 59: For cross-country riding, protection is needed for both pony and rider. A young rider models two forms of protective wear. **Top left and right** the jockey skull cap, fitted with a chin strap and over which a plain or coloured silk is worn, and the back protector, which goes under the jersey or jacket. Back protectors come in various shapes but their aim is to guard the spine and ribs from injury. **Bottom** A surcingle should be put on over the saddle as a safeguard against accidents should the girth break. The reins are rubber-covered to prevent the rider's hands from slipping. The pony has all four legs bandaged to protect him against raps and tendon injury.

Always undo all plaiting as soon as you have finished the classes in which plaits are needed. Use small, sharp, pointed scissors – embroidery scissors are best – and snip the threads carefully, making certain that you do not cut the hair at the same time.

TYPES OF SHOW

Show-jumping

Most local shows hold show-jumping competitions, usually restricted to competitors of a certain age or ponies of a certain height. Novice competitions are generally open to combinations (that is, pony and rider together) who have not won a jumping event. Other novice classes are described as £10 Novice or £30 Novice. This means that the total winnings of the combination must not exceed that amount. So, even if you have had some success already, you may still be eligible for a novice event. All these classes are described as *unaffiliated* and, although they are usually judged by the rules of the British Show Jumping Association (BSJA), there may be local variations. Prize money cannot exceed an amount stipulated by the BSJA.

Affiliated classes are quite a different matter. To be eligible to compete in affiliated shows, you must be a paid up member of the British Show Jumping Association and your pony must be registered with the BSJA. Novice ponies are registered JC (Junior Grade C) but will be upgraded to JA (Junior Grade A) when their winnings reach a certain figure. The jumps in these classes will be of a stipulated height, and the speed at which the course should be jumped is also laid down. If you are not a member of the BSJA, even if you buy a registered jumping pony, you cannot compete in affiliated shows.

In the USA some shows are affiliated with the American Horse Shows Association (AHSA); others that are not are called 'non-recognized' shows. Novice classes in the USA are referred to as 'green' or 'maiden' events. Novice ponies competing in AHSA recognized shows are also classified by their earnings. The Preliminary horse will be upgraded to an Intermediate horse, once his earnings have reached a certain level.

Working hunter pony

Classes for working hunter ponies (WHP) have become very popular in recent years. They were started in response to a demand for some type of showing class for ponies which would carry their young riders safely out hunting and were nice-looking ponies although not quite good enough for purely showing events.

Competitors in these classes start off by jumping a course of natural fences – not coloured ones – and those which have not been eliminated in the jumping phase are then judged on conformation. Although, as in any showing class, the result depends on the opinion of the judges, a nice, forward-going pony which jumps the course confidently and willingly should have the edge on a pony which may be beautiful to look at but is an unwilling or hesitant jumper. There are usually five separate WHP classes: Cradle Stakes, for ponies 12 hh and under, ridden by children aged nine years and under; Nursery Stakes, for ponies exceeding 12 hh but not exceeding 13 hh, ridden by children aged eleven years and under; 13 hh and under, riders fourteen years and under; over 13 hh but not exceeding 14 hh, riders sixteen and under; over 14 hh but not exceeding 15 hh, riders eighteen and under.

A recently-introduced show category is the class for ponies of hunter type. The ponies are similar to WHP entries but are not asked to complete a jumping course.

Hunter trials

These are cross-country events, in which riders have to complete a course of fixed fences at a fair hunting pace. There is often a timed section, with a gate to be opened and closed. The winner is not necessarily the fastest, as most hunter trials have what is known as a bogey time, which is not revealed to the competitors but which is worked out by

Pages 62–3 A typical cross-country fence, well ridden. **Top left** The horse approaches the fence, the rider having previously walked the course and settled on the best line. **Bottom left** As the horse lands, the rider is already looking towards the next fence. **Right** A clean, neat turn. The rider's weight is well forward to free the pony's loins and encourage speed.

the organizers according to the length of the course. Time penalties are given to those riders who exceed or fall short of the time allowed, and are added to any penalties gathered during the round. Penalties are given for refusals (three refusals at any one jump usually means elimination) and for falls while tackling a jump. A fall in between fences is not penalized. In pairs events, where two competitors ride round the course together, there are generally two or three dressing fences which the riders must take abreast, and they will earn penalties if they are not together. At some hunter trials, marks for style are also given. Competitors in hunter trials are expected to wear tweed jackets, although they may wear crash helmets with dark blue or black silk hat covers.

Competitors wear bibs with their number printed on, so that the number can be seen clearly by the fence judges. You will usually be asked for a small deposit when you collect your numbered bib, which you get back when you return your number. You should always check, when you collect your number, whether you will be riding in numerical order or whether you have to declare at the start. If the latter, this means that you give your number to the starter's steward who will enter it on a list on a blackboard. Always allow yourself plenty of time to warm up before the start.

One-day events

The one-day event consists of three disciplines: dressage, cross-country and show-jumping. Usually the show-jumping phase follows the cross-country, but this depends on the organizers. The dressage phase is always first.

The dressage phase The dressage test to be used will be given on the schedule, and a copy of the test can usually be obtained from the organizers. When you make your entry, you may be asked to enclose a stamped addressed envelope so that your dressage time may be sent to you, or you may have to telephone the organizers a day or two before the event. The time given to you may seem rather odd: 11.14 a.m., for example, or 12.08 p.m. The reason for this precision is that organizers allow seven minutes per competitor (five minutes for the test and two minutes for the judge to write up any comments).

Dress for the dressage test is: jacket, tie, velvet-covered hard hat. Present yourself to the dressage steward at least ten minutes before your test is due and spend the intervening period walking your pony round quietly. When the competitor before you leaves the dressage arena, the steward will indicate that it is now your turn. This does not mean that you immediately rush into the arena but simply that you should start walking your pony quietly round the perimeter of the arena on the outside, thus showing to the judge that you are ready to begin when invited to. The signal to start may be a bell or a car horn. When you hear it, you continue round the arena until you reach the entrance at the marker 'A'.

In Pony Club dressage tests – and these include one-day events – certain rules are laid down. You cannot, for example, ride your pony in a double bridle; a snaffle should be worn, although a drop noseband or martingale is acceptable. The rider may carry a whip but is not allowed to wear spurs. The pony may not be shown in leg bandages, brushing boots or overreach boots. You must wear a crash helmet.

In dressage, each part of the test is marked out of ten, and the marks gained are totalled and taken away from the maximum score. The figure obtained is your dressage score and the lower it is, the better.

The cross-country phase In some one-day events, you will be given a starting time for the cross-country phase, and for the show-jumping. There will always be plenty of time for you to change out of your dressage clothes and into your cross-country clothing. Most people like to ride in colours, a striped rugby shirt or jersey, with complementary coloured silk for the crash helmet. Wear the best protective clothing available, such as a proper crash helmet with chin strap, and a back protector. The latter is made of expanded polystyrene, often reinforced down the centre, and it is intended to protect the spine in case of a bad fall. The design of the back protector is improved from time to time. Some back protectors are curved to guard against rib injuries and to protect the base of the spine. It is held in position by a strap around the waist and is worn under the shirt or jersey.

The pony should also wear some sort of protective clothing, such as overreach boots and or leg bandages. A cross-country surcingle which passes over the saddle and round the pony's girth is a useful safety measure against the saddle girths suddenly breaking. The surcingle has an elasticated inset to stop it from restricting the pony's movements.

The show-jumping phase The rider should change back into jacket and tie. Formal dress should always be worn for the prize-giving, if you are lucky or skilful enough to get into the rosettes.

Combined training

This competition consists of two phases: dressage and show-jumping. The dressage phase always takes place first.

CHAPTER 7
Choosing your first horse

Choice of horse is, perhaps, even more important than choice of pony. The capital cost of a horse is likely to be three, four or even five times that of a pony, and when you are spending thousands rather than hundreds, mistakes are expensive. But there is a more subtle reason. Someone switching from ponies to horses is usually acknowledging that he or she intends to carry on riding, that what has been a pleasant pastime is now worthy of a more serious approach, and that they may even make a career with or relating to horses.

One of the first things you have to decide is whether you are looking for a 'made' horse or for one which you can train yourself. It depends on your attitude. A highly-competitive rider may prefer to take over a horse which has already proved itself in the show-ring. Another may prefer training a horse to competing, but this calls for a patient temperament and plenty of spare time.

Made horses will clearly cost more to buy than a young horse or a green one. To buy an unschooled horse with potential is more of a gamble, but provided that your judgement is sound it is more satisfying than following in someone else's successful footsteps.

So be honest with yourself. Examine your motives carefully and look ahead as far as you can. Is this a short-term project? If you are approaching the gap between school and college, are you looking for one short successful season? Will you, in a year or eighteen months' time, still have the energy, desire and hours available to continue your horse's schooling programme? Bear in mind that what was true for ponies – namely that it can take six months, a year or even longer for rider and pony to build up a really good relationship – is just as true for horses.

One of the most important facts to remember is that a horse is not just a large pony. Most ponies, even those of indeterminate breed, have sufficient native blood in their veins to respond happily to little work or lots. They are fairly easy to keep since most of them will live out, and need a less arduous routine to make them fit enough to take part in competiton.

Horses, most of whom have some Thoroughbred in their ancestry, are much greedier of your time and attention. They certainly cannot winter out, even though they may live out during the summer months. Because they are physically bigger, everything connected with them is more expensive. Shoeing bills, for example, are likely to be higher and to occur more often. They eat more food, their worming dosages are higher, and items of tack and clothing are dearer.

If you settled for a small stable when you had a pony, you will now be faced with finding or building a bigger loose box. If you have a small pony trailer, you now need one capable of carrying a horse in safety and comfort. A bigger trailer, with a heavier occupant, may require a bigger car.

Examine all the pros and cons carefully, find out as much as you can from friends with horses, talk it over with your parents – and then decide. The ways of finding a horse are no different from finding a pony. Word-of-mouth, advertisements, or a dealer are the principal sources of horses for sale. It is mainly the purchase price that changes.

WHAT TYPE OF HORSE?

Many riders aged seventeen plus, who, as associate members of the Pony Club, are still eligible to take part in Pony Club activities and compete in Pony Club competitions and team events, are looking for a horse which is capable of taking them over the bigger courses found in competitions at this level. By this age, they have usually decided on the type of riding they most enjoy and are often prepared to work harder than younger children to achieve their goal.

In an event like the tetrathlon, for example, which comprises the four disciplines: shooting, swimming, riding and running, a great deal of effort will be put into improving performance in the shooting, swimming and running phases. But if the pony cannot tackle the cross-country course, which although not difficult does have obstacles up to a height of 1.07 m (3 ft 6 in), much of that effort will have been wasted. So a young tetrathlon enthusiast will be looking for a horse on which she can approach the cross-country phase with confidence.

Fences in show-jumping and eventing competitions are also higher at Pony Club associate level, while the keen dressage competitor may be anxious to progress to the more advanced tests.

There is often, too, a desire to improve for improvement's sake and to feel that progress is not only possible but being achieved.

For the really keen young rider, there is enormous satisfaction to be gained in taking an untrained horse and building up his confidence and experience gradually until, some eighteen months or two years later, he can be truly described as a polished performer. Or, if you want to look even further ahead, you might wish to start with an unbroken youngster and bring him to the peak of his potential entirely yourself.

BREEDS OF HORSE

The riding horse is not as easy to define, in terms of breeding, as the mountain or moorland pony. For example, with the nine breeds of pony indigenous to the British Isles very clear rules are laid down by the breed societies and cover such characteristics as height, colour, markings and shape. A horse, however, is roughly defined as standing more than 14.2 hh at the withers; and a riding horse is one which is a comfortable ride.

Many of today's riding horses have an ancestry in which such varied types as Thoroughbred, Arab, carriage horse, draught horse and native pony are combined. The Hunters' Improvement Society has, in the hundred years since it was formed, made great efforts to establish a good hunter type, principally by its Premium Schemes for stallions and mares and by organizing important shows.

The qualities required by a good hunter are a calm temperament, boldness, strength and stamina. These will stand it in good stead in the hunting field, where it may be called upon to stand around for long periods, gallop for long stretches, tackle big or tricky fences in muddy or hard going, in and out of woods, and possibly to keep going for several hours. These qualities are also of value in the show-jumping arena and the eventing field.

The hunter should have a deep, wide chest, with plenty of heart room, short back and sloping shoulder, strong muscular loins and quarters. Its legs must be clean and strong, with good bone, knees large, hocks large and bony. Its hooves should be big and open, with hard horn and a well-developed frog. The head must be lean, small-muzzled and well-boned, with a bold but kindly eye.

The deeper the girth and the bigger the bone (that is, the circumference of the leg measured just below the knee), the greater the weight the horse is able to carry.

Some of the best hunters have been half-breeds; by a Thoroughbred stallion out of a draught mare, the first for speed and quality, the second for strength. Cross-breeding, however, has produced a variety of types, and in recent years many of the Continental breeds have become popular for dressage, show-jumping and eventing. Of these, the German Hanoverian is one of the most liked, possibly because it seems to have an inbred love of competition and showmanship, although it was originally bred as a carriage horse.

Page 67 Riding out for relaxation. A rider usually makes the change from pony to horse because he or she intends to take a more serious approach to what was previously a hobby – probably by moving on to a higher level of competition. However, it is important to continue to enjoy the pleasures of riding as well.

In fact, it is the carriage horses of the past which are much in demand today for all forms of competition: the English Cleveland Bay, the German Oldenburg and Trakehner, the Dutch Gelderland, the Swiss Einsiedler, and many others. Ireland, where the Irish or English Thoroughbred was first crossed with a draught mare to produce a fine hunter, still breeds some of the best horses in the world.

The Arab horse has fanatical support throughout the world. Pure-bred Arab studs can be found in many countries, and the Arab-Thoroughbred cross, known as the Anglo-Arab, combines the qualities of both, particularly the beauty and presence of the Arab with the extra height and speed of the Thoroughbred.

In the USA, many of the individual saddle-horse breeds have been developed with a particular purpose in mind. The Quarter Horse, for example, capable of the short bursts of speed and extreme agility which are necessary in controlling cattle, is an unrivalled cow-pony. Some of the saddle horses from the southern states, the Tennessee Walking Horse or Kentucky Saddler, have additional gaits which are very comfortable and showy. Others are bred for their markings: the Appaloosa or the Pinto, for example.

Most of the horses used for show-jumping and eventing in the USA are descended from horses imported from Europe during the twentieth century, mostly from the British Isles, but increasingly from Germany as well.

Page 70 A horse and rider going well in a cross-country event. A great deal of time and dedication is needed to look after a horse that is going to be ridden in competitions such as two- and three-day events.

CHAPTER 8
Careers with horses

When you have owned a horse for a year or two, you will know whether riding for you is always going to be just a hobby, or whether you would like to earn a living working with horses.

Many young people go through a stage of wanting to work with horses. For most, it is never more than a stage. Other interests gradually take over until eventually they give up riding altogether. They never lose their

Working with horses demands the qualities of patience and calmness, together with physical courage and strength. Here the horse is being lunged, which improves suppleness and teaches obedience.

love of horses, of course, and are likely to become involved again when their own children are old enough to enjoy ponies, but for the time being horses take a back seat.

If, however, you are seriously interested in working with horses, you should first examine the different careers available, finding out what qualifications are required, what the work involves and how you can best prepare yourself to enter the profession. You should also examine your own character as honestly as you can.

PERSONAL QUALITIES

Working with any animal requires patience, calmness, kindness and a highly developed sense of responsibility. Working with horses may also require physical courage.

Ask yourself various questions. Are you the type who gets in a flap when things go wrong? Can you be firm when necessary? Do you mind working at all hours? Will you cheerfully turn out when the weather is wet and windy?

Another requirement is that you should be physically healthy and reasonably strong. There is nothing like lugging a few bales of hay about or raking over the surface of an all-weather school to leave you feeling wrung out and ready to drop. It is even worse when you know that you still have half a dozen horses to muck out, feed and get ready for the night.

Hard work is part of any career with horses. Even if you become a top show-jumper, life will not consist just of being a superstar at Wembley, handing your horse to a groom and signing countless autographs. Even the top show-jumpers spend a great deal of time training, bringing on young horses and, probably most tedious of all, travelling.

Nevertheless, there is a great deal of satisfaction to be had from working with horses and sometimes good financial rewards as well. There are also many different ways to make a living on the equestrian scene.

RIDING INSTRUCTOR

In order to teach riding, a person must hold one of the British Horse Society's qualifying certificates, which are awarded to students passing the relevant examinations. These qualifications are: the Assistant Instructor's, which entitles the holder to put the letters BHSAI after their name; the Intermediate Instructor's (BHSII); the Instructor's (BHSI); and the Fellowship of the British Horse Society (FBHS). There is a minimum age limit for each examination: seventeen-and-a-half years for the BHSAI, twenty-two years for the BHSI, and twenty-five years for the Fellowship. Minimum GCE or CSE requirements are four O-levels or four Grade 1 passes at CSE, except for those who are twenty years or over when they start the course.

Because the British Horse Society is recognized as a responsible body for setting and maintaining standards of riding and teaching, further education grants may be available from county educational authorities for any student wishing to enrol on a course.

Training may take place at any recognized establishment and can be done either as a working pupil or as a fee-paying student. Training usually lasts a year in the case of a working pupil, sometimes less when the tuition is paid for.

GROOM

A groom may be solely responsible for looking after someone's horses, or be part of a large stable. He or she should, of course, know all about horse management and be able to exercise many different horses. They should know how to get a horse fit, and how to prepare him for a show. In addition, it helps to be able to drive.

A groom's work can be very hard and is often poorly paid. Unscrupulous employers rely on their grooms' dedication to the horses in their care and are not above exploiting them quite shamelessly. A good employer, however, can make a groom's life extremely pleasant. For example, to work for a leading show-jumper or eventer can provide a life of constant variety and excitement.

The BHS Horsemastership examination or the Groom's Diploma offered by the Association of British Riding Schools provides the paper qualifications necessary to be a groom. For the former, the syllabus is the same as that laid down for the BHSAI, but without the teaching. For the latter, a minimum of eighteen months' full-time work with horses is required, and the entrant must be at least seventeen-and-a-half years old when taking the examination. The Groom's Diploma is recognized in most countries as evidence of competence.

The BHS also offers a Stable Manager's

Certificate, which qualifies the holder to manage or own any kind of yard, and to train student grooms. Preparation for this certificate also covers the business side of stable management.

RACING

There are two types of racing; flat racing and National Hunt racing. The latter takes place over jumps; either steeplechase jumps or hurdles. In the UK, both flat racing and National Hunt racing are under the control of the Jockey Club. The most valuable horses, and the greatest prizes and prestige, are found in flat racing.

In both cases, racehorses are kept at training establishments, where they are looked after by 'lads', who in many cases are actually 'lasses'. A lad is a lad whatever his or her age, from a youngster just out of school up to the Head Lad, who is quite possibly a grandparent.

Lads are the stable staff, who are responsible for the feeding, grooming and mucking-out of the horses in their care. They may or may not ride the horses out to exercise, depending on their own wishes and the policy of the individual trainer.

Aspiring flat jockeys are called apprentices. They are contracted to stay with a particular stable for three, five or seven years. Like the lads, apprentices 'do' two or three horses in the yard, looking after them entirely themselves, riding them out to exercise and travelling with them when they go racing.

An apprentice might not ride in an actual race for as much as a year after joining a stable. Flat meetings often have special races for apprentices, and that may be the first opportunity to don proper silks and appear in public on a real racecourse. However, an apprentice who is a particularly good rider may be entered in other races, especially if, by doing so, the trainer can claim a weight allowance. Racehorses carry a stipulated weight according to their ability. Obviously, the more weight a horse has to carry, the greater his disadvantage over other horses in a race. However, a young jockey's inexperience is counter-balanced by the fact that his or her mount carries less weight. If an apprentice wins a few races, the allowance is reduced accordingly, until eventually no allowance at all is given.

In a flat-racing training stables, the horses will be much younger than those found in a National Hunt stables. Horses are allowed to start racing at two years old, and many trainers break in young horses when they are about eighteen months old. Apprentices who are very light, small-boned but strong, may well be asked to help with the breaking in, and will be taught how to lunge and to back young horses.

Many National Hunt horses began with flat racing, and later switched to jumping. Consistent winners on the flat are usually retired to stud by the age of four or five years. However, some of the less brilliant ones will be tried over hurdles and later perhaps steeplechase fences, especially if they show stamina rather than speed.

The financial rewards for leading flat jockeys are very great indeed, but only about one in ten apprentices manages to become a jockey, and of these only a very few reach the top.

But a lad's work can be satisfying, especially for those who take pride in turning out a horse at the peak of fitness and appearance. Most lads become very attached to the horses in their care – and vice versa – and nowhere are patience, understanding, and gentleness more valuable than in dealing with skittish young Thoroughbreds.

STUD WORK

This is one of the most rewarding careers, and it is extremely important work. Good handling of a foal is absolutely vital to producing a kind temperament in the adult horse. A horse's life-long attitude to human beings depends on its early introduction to the way in which human beings behave. Patience allied to firmness is essential in anyone dealing with brood mares and their offspring.

The National Pony Society offers a Stud Assistant's Certificate, followed by a Diploma in stud work. Both are awarded as a result of fairly stiff practical examinations. Trainees at a stud learn how to manage, handle and look

Page 74 A farrier at work. A farrier's job is highly skilled; it requires knowledge not only of how to make and put on shoes, but also of the horses movement, the ways in which shoeing can correct faulty action and balance, and of diseases of the foot. The training involves a four-year apprenticeship.
Page 75 The training for a veterinary surgeon lasts for five years. A vet who wishes to work with horses will need to practise in an area with a large equine population. A veterinary training can also lead on to working in equine research.

after stallions and brood mares; and about the feeding and weaning of foals. They are taught how to handle young ponies, and how to lunge and back them; how to prepare for and present animals in the show-ring; and how to train young horses under the saddle.

Someone who is interested in bloodstock breeding – that is, the breeding and raising of Thoroughbreds – should seek advice from the Thoroughbred Breeders' Association as to which studs are willing to accept students.

HUNT SERVICE

Anyone who enjoys hunting tends to think of it as a sport to be paid for, and forgets that there are people who earn their livelihood in the hunting world. The principal employee of a hunt is the Huntsman, who, quite apart from hunting hounds, is in charge of the hunt stables and the hunt kennels. The Kennel Huntsman looks after the field when the Master is not hunting, and is answerable to the Huntsman. Whippers-in may be amateurs, but most are paid employees and the positions of First Whipper-in and Second Whipper-in represent stepping stones on the way to becoming a huntsman. Under the Second Whipper-in is the Second Horseman, who takes charge of the hunt horses at a meet, while under him are the various grooms and stable boys employed in the stables.

This type of job is definitely for the country-lover, and for someone who has the patience and love of animals that any work with horses requires. In addition, hunt servants need tact when dealing with people: they are ambassadors for the hunt whenever they appear in public, and must be able to keep their tempers even when provoked.

Openings in hunt work are clearly limited in number. There is no examination, and no official qualification. A visit to the local kennels for a chat with the huntsman may be the best means of starting in this type of work. If there are no openings locally, the huntsman may know of vacancies in other hunts.

FARRIER

The farrier is the one person with whom every horse-owner is likely to get acquainted. You will have visited the farrier – or the farrier you – at least six times a year ever since you acquired your first pony. You may have had more than one farrier during that time, and if you held your pony each time his feet were attended to, you will have had plenty of opportunity to watch a farrier at work.

The farrier is one of the most important people in a horse's life. Without the knowledge and skill they bring to their work, a horse would be incapable of carrying out the tasks expected of him. A careless farrier can lame a horse for life. Badly-fitted shoes, incorrectly trimmed feet, or nails driven home without thought, can all make a horse unsound. Think of the weight that a horse's feet have to bear; in some activities, such as jumping or galloping, there is a moment when all that weight is carried by one foot alone.

There was a time when every village had its forge. When machines replaced horses on the roads and in agriculture, the farrier's profession declined. But the growing popularity of riding for leisure increased the demand again, and although the village smithy has not made a comeback the farrier certainly has.

Modern farriers are much more mobile than their predecessors. They still need a forge, complete with fire and anvil, in which to make shoes, but it is no longer essential for them to shoe horses alongside it. Now, they carry their tools with them and travel to their clients by car. If hot shoeing is required, they may have a portable forge, but many farriers offer only a cold shoeing service and still have more customers than they can deal with.

Farriers need to know more than how to make shoes and to put them on. They must understand the way a horse's limbs work, especially the tendons and joints, and how they are affected by the shape of the hoof. They must know about diseases of the foot and the remedies that they can apply. They must be aware of what they can do to correct faulty action or to improve a horse's balance.

With so much knowledge needed, it follows that training takes a long time. It involves being apprenticed to a master farrier for four years, and attending courses, during this time, in farriery at special schools approved by the Worshipful Company of Farriers. At the end of this training, there is an examination; and those who are successful become Registered Shoeing Smiths and can set up in business. Later on, further qualifications can be added; by becoming an Associate of the Farriery Company of London, or a Fellow of the Worshipful Company of Farriers.

VETERINARY SURGEON

A vet's training takes as long as that of a doctor: five years at any of the six veterinary colleges in the UK. At least three good A-level passes in scientific subjects are needed to win a place, and competition is very keen.

The training includes a certain amount of practical work; such as working on a farm and, in the three years before the final examinations, as a student in a veterinary practice. The course leads to a bachelor's degree, Bachelor of Veterinary Medicine and Surgery, (BVMS), and then to Membership of the Royal College of Veterinary Surgeons (MRCVS). Post-graduate work can lead to doctorates in veterinary medicine and surgery, and to a Fellowship of the Royal College (FRCVS).

A newly-qualified vet may join an existing practice; first as an assistant, and later, if good enough, as a partner. On the other hand, some people prefer to go into veterinary research, or to enter the civil service and work for the Ministry of Agriculture.

There can be no guarantee, of course, that a vet's work will include horses, although they are bound to be among the patients of a country practice. Those who prefer to deal with horses rather than other animals, should try to join a practice in an area with a large equine population; if possible, one that includes several racing stables. It may be possible eventually to build up a reputation as an equine specialist whose services are greatly in demand; but no one can say at the start of their training that they wish to deal with horses alone.

Those whose interest lies in research should aim to work, eventually, for the Newmarket Equine Research Station, where all manner of horse diseases and problems are investigated.

VETERINARY NURSE

Those who wish to have a career caring for sick animals, but do not have the necessary qualifications to train as a veterinary surgeon, can join the veterinary profession as a nurse, becoming a Registered Animal Nursing Auxiliary (RANA). Nurses, like veterinary surgeons, cannot opt to work just with horses.

RANA trainees must be at least seventeen years old when they start, and will need three O-levels; in English, and either mathematics or physical or biological science. The training consists of working as a nurse with a professional veterinary surgeon, and attending lectures at college when required. Courses include animal anatomy and physiology; and anaesthesia, so that the nurse can assist a veterinary surgeon during an operation.

OTHER WORK CONNECTED WITH HORSES

If none of the jobs so far mentioned interests you sufficiently, but you would still like a career connected with horses, you might like to work in a saddlers. All over the country, there are numerous saddlery shops where a young assistant can gain a great deal of satisfaction from selling tack and other equipment. Many of these shops take their goods in mobile vans around to the shows; even quite small shows have a number of trade stands these days.

With a certain amount of capital behind you, you could even start up on your own, although it would be wise to work for a time in someone else's shop first, to learn the business and get to know the representatives of the various manufacturers.

If you are interested in saddlery, you could seek an apprenticeship with a Master Saddler, where for a period of about five years you would learn the craft of leather-working and saddle-making.

Another field in which a knowledge of horses and riding can provide a good living is in buying and selling horses. The most important quality in this work is honesty. A dealer's reputation goes before him and the surest road to ruin is to attribute non-existent virtues to a horse in order to make a quick sale. However, dealers who do their best to find a suitable animal for a client, and who can tell, better than the client can, what exactly he or she wants, are always in great demand.

Whatever career you decide upon, always try to find out as much about it as you can. Almost all the professions mentioned are open to boys and girls, with the possible ex-

Pages 78–9 An instructor at work: holding the pony of a young pupil, while he mounts unaided; and keeping a watchful eye on a class of young riders.

ception of hunt servants, but some jobs are inevitably more suitable for people with physical strength, others for those of small stature. A pint-sized adult with a flair for riding, for example, could be just the person to break in riding ponies for children, but the same person would not have the physical strength to be a vet in a large-animal practice.

If you intend to start your own business, it would be sensible to attend a course in business studies. Learn how to type, how to make VAT returns and to prepare a profit and loss account, and you will be well equipped to deal with the often boring but necessary paperwork that business management involves. And, of course, learn to drive. Almost any work, from being a groom to running a saddlers, is made easier if you can drive a car.

CHAPTER 9

Mainly for parents

From the moment you become a pony-owner to the time you have grown up, your parents will be your partners in the pony-owning venture. Even if they know nothing at all about horses at the outset, they will over the years become very knowledgeable, because there is no way in which they can avoid being involved. This section gives them some idea of what they are getting involved in.

At the beginning, a parent's involvement is principally financial. It is unrealistic to expect any child to be able to pay the costs of looking after a pony all by herself. Even if you own a field, the upkeep of a pony can run into several pounds a week.

The cost is not spread evenly throughout the year. In summer, when a pony is feeding almost solely on grass, he is cheap to keep. In winter, hay and concentrates soon run up big bills at the corn-chandlers. Shoeing expenses crop up every eight weeks or so, and veterinary bills – even for routine things like worming powders and anti-tetanus and anti-flu vaccinations – add to the annual cost.

You can be sure that, whatever a pony has – in the way of saddlery, grooming kits, clothing, and so on – his young owner will always think that he needs more. Anti-sweat rugs, summer sheets, tail bandages, leg bandages, travelling bandages, tail guards, rubber reins, drop nosebands, grooming kit boxes, buckets, haynets, fly fringes; the list never gets any shorter. Hoof-picks are forever getting lost and have to be replaced; saddles need re-stuffing from time to time; whips vanish into thin air.

The rider grows and needs new clothes: jodhpur boots fall apart, one pair of jodhpurs is superseded by two, three, even four or five pairs, a tweed jacket is joined by a showing jacket.

The Pony Club subscription comes up once a year. Show entry fees, which are quite small while the rider is still on the leading rein, get more expensive as pony and rider progress to bigger and better competitions.

Competitions, in turn, lead to even more expense. The velvet-covered riding hat is fine for gymkhanas, but once a child starts entering Pony Club events, she will need a proper crash hat, and for cross-country riding a back protector and a rugby shirt in her chosen colours.

INSURANCE

A pony is a valuable animal; it is also a living creature subject to illness and accidents, sometimes fatal. It should be regarded as an investment, and protected as such.

There are a number of insurance policies on the market, advertised in the horse magazines. All that is necessary is to choose the most suitable, fill in the proposal form on the advertisement, enclose a cheque for the premium, and post it off. Alternatively, insurance can be arranged through a broker.

Policies are usually graded to cater for different needs. Basic insurance will provide cover against loss or injury incurred during ordinary hacking and Pony Club events. Some activities, such as hunting, attract higher premiums. There are clauses covering veterinary fees, permanent disablement of the animal, and theft of the pony. Saddlery can be covered. And a trailer can be insured for a small extra premium. Personal liability is

included in all policies. This provides cover against claims arising from injury to a third party caused by your pony. Most policies have an excess clause.

TRAILERS

Once a child regularly takes part in competitions, the question of whether to buy a trailer or horse-box will arise.

In the past, it was quite usual for young competitors to attend all the shows within a 12-mile radius of their homes without using a horse-box. Today however, motorways and busy roads have made hacking any distance a risky business. And it is unreasonable to expect a keenly competitive child to be content with the few shows which are close enough to be reached on horseback.

It may be possible to beg a lift from time to time in someone else's trailer, but friends, however obliging, may not always be going to the same event. Even if they are, your classes and theirs may not coincide. One or other of you will be kept hanging about, either having to arrive too early or leave too late. It is possible to hire a trailer, but sooner or later, you will probably decide to buy one.

Always buy the best trailer you can afford. Trailers range in size from those which can take two ponies, to those big enough for two 17.2 hh horses. Single-sized trailers are available, but most horses and ponies travel better with a companion, and to take someone else's pony in your trailer will add very little to the expense.

A trailer with a front-unload (that is, fitted with a front ramp as well as a rear one) is heavier than one with a rear ramp only. On the other hand, it is easier and safer to lead a horse forwards out of the trailer than to back him down a rear ramp. It is also easier to get a shy loader into a front-unload trailer.

The floor is particularly important as this is the part which is likely to rot. It should be made of hardwood, preferably with a 3 mm ($\frac{1}{8}$ in) gap between the planks so that urine can drain easily and air can circulate to speed up the drying. The lighting system should work properly; side and tail-lights, braking lights and indicators are operated from the towing vehicle. If possible have the wheel bearings examined.

A double-axle trailer is more stable than one with only a single axle. Inspect the tyres carefully, especially the tyre walls. Since a trailer often spends more time parked than in use, the tyre treads are likely to wear less quickly than the tyre walls.

Inside, most trailers have padding on the side walls and a central, removable partition, which may be no more than a single bar secured fore and aft by a vertical pillar. Partitions which reach to the floor should be padded. There are usually detachable breast bars and jockey straps.

Some trailers are fitted with non-slip matting on the ramps, which deadens the sound as the pony is being loaded.

Second-hand trailers are advertised regularly in magazines and local papers. If you buy a second-hand trailer, the points to look at are the condition of the floor; the state of the lighting system; the ease of raising and lowering the ramps; the brakes and wheels. If possible, have the trailer examined by an expert before buying it.

TOWING VEHICLES

Most trailers can be towed quite easily by a family car with an engine capacity of 2,000 cc. A tow-bar will be needed on the car. Four-wheel drive vehicles are at an advantage in wet weather conditions.

TOWING A TRAILER

Of all the duties that a pony-owning parent is expected to fulfil, to tow a trailer with horses inside is the one which causes the most apprehension. Yet many do so regularly without mishap.

If you have never towed a trailer before, start by taking it out on the road when it is empty. An empty trailer is not exactly like a full one, but it will give you an idea of how your car behaves with a trailer behind it and you can practise starting, stopping, and

Pages 82–83 Loading. A pony is more willing to follow if the handler walks quietly into the box without looking at him. This pony has confidence, but difficult loaders may be cured of their problems if a front unload trailer is used and the front ramp lowered. Coconut matting on the loading ramps will help to deaden noise.

turning corners without having to worry about any passengers.

Practise reversing as well. This can cause all sorts of difficulties, so it is wise to master the technique as soon as possible. It may help to have a look at the way a toy Land-Rover and trailer work, provided the toy has movable front wheels operated by the steering wheel. It will show you exactly what the trailer does when you steer the towing vehicle. The trailer acts in an opposite fashion to the car. In other words, if you wish the trailer to bend to the right, you turn the car's steering wheel to the left, reversing the wheel only when the movement has been established. Try it out a few times with the toy trailer on the carpet.

Once on the road with a loaded trailer, you should aim to give the occupants as smooth a ride as possible. This means early anticipation of changes of direction and speed. Remember that your stopping distances are increased by the weight of the trailer, and start changing to a lower gear well before you reach a road junction so that you can come to a stop without any unnecessary jerk. You should also move off as smoothly as possible, taking time to go through the gears.

Take corners slightly wider than you would if you were driving the car by itself, to allow for the extra width of the trailers, and at crossroads bear in mind the extra length of car and trailer combined.

If you are taking only one horse or pony in a double trailer, the animal will have a better journey if he is loaded into the right-hand side. With two ponies of different sizes, travel with the bigger one on the outside.

The speed at which you travel depends on the nature of the road. Although 50 mph (80 km/h) is the legal limit, it is better to keep the speed to a maximum of 40 mph (64 km/h). The time lost on a journey of 10 miles (16 km) is only a few minutes, and it is better to set off early and arrive with a pair of calm ponies, than to drive as fast as possible thereby flustering the ponies.

Finally, remember other road-users. There is nothing more frustrating for other drivers than to be stuck behind a trailer with no hope of passing it safely. So if you are on a narrow road and the traffic behind you is building up, pull into a lay-by when you see one and allow the cars to pass. You will waste only a minute or two at the most, but you will be making a worthwhile contribution to road safety.

LOADING AND UNLOADING A PONY

A horse or pony which walks quietly into a trailer first time, with no fuss, is a joy to own. Most ponies load quite willingly, but there are always a few who, through sheer naughtiness, like to make a fuss.

If this is the case with your horse, and as long as you are satisfied that the animal is not frightened, you have to be firm. Often, just the production of a lunge-line or whip will do the trick. A lunge-line is connected to one side of the trailer ramp, brought round to the other side behind the horse and gradually tightened around his hindquarters. Coupled with a firm leader at the animal's head, the extra pressure should be sufficient to persuade him to enter the trailer.

If this fails because the horse swings his rear end off the trailer ramp, you will need extra help. Two lunge-lines crossed behind his quarters, with a strong person on each end, may provide the necessary compulsion. A further line, clipped to his headcollar and passing through a ring inside the trailer at the front, with the free end coming back out of the trailer alongside the horse, where a third assistant can apply steady pressure, is the next method to try.

Sometimes a horse just likes to take his time. If he likes to stand still and take a look around between each step, you will have to allow him to do this. Any sign of impatience will build up his resistance, whereas left to himself, he will probably walk quietly into the trailer eventually. You will just have to allow as much time as is needed before each journey. Greedy animals may be tempted into a trailer by the offer of food; other horses will load only if their companion has entered first. In every case, get to know your horse in order to find the best way of tackling any problem.

If your trailer has a front ramp it is quite simple to unload the horse. The handler gets into the trailer and removes the front bar. As soon as she is ready, the assistant outside lowers the ramp and the pony is led forwards from the trailer. When lowering the ramp, stand slightly to one side to avoid being knocked down or injured if the pony decides to make his exit at a run.

Unloading backwards is slightly more hazardous, as the jockey strap under the horse's hindquarters cannot be undone until the ramp is down. If a horse always rushes

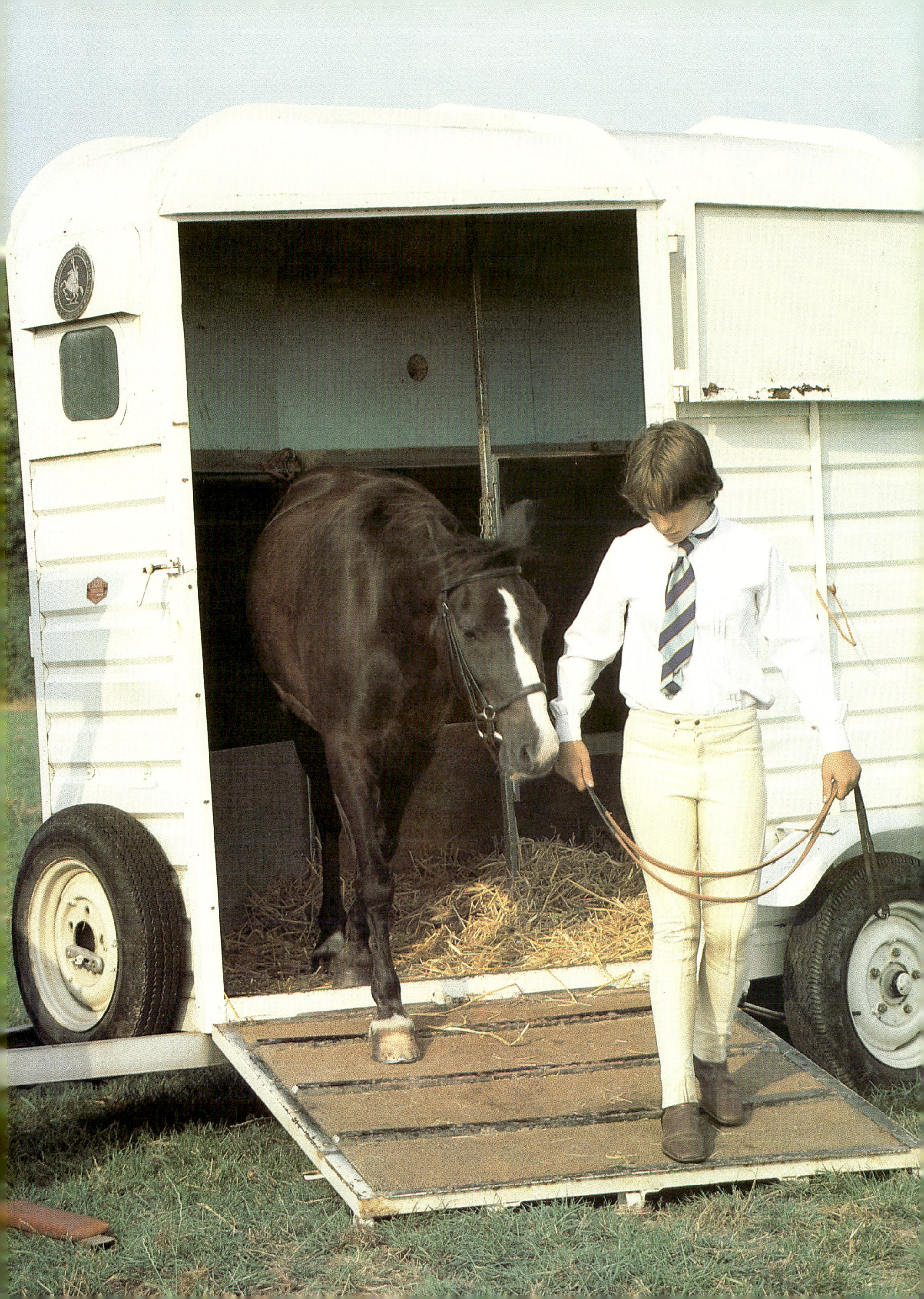

out very quickly, it is best not to use the jockey strap at all.

The handler should always talk to the horse in a soothing way, whether the animal is being unloaded frontwards or backwards.

PARTING WITH A PONY

At various stages through your child's riding career, you will be faced with the distress caused by parting with a much-loved pony. It is best if the old pony goes while the child is at school. There is bound to be a certain amount of grief, but excitement over the replacement will soon ease the pain. The process is easier when you already have a new pony to take the place of the previous one.

However, the main concern at this time is the question of finding a good home for the pony. If you can inspect his new premises and meet the family of the new owner, your fears should be allayed. But, of course, once you have actually accepted a cheque for the pony, he is no longer your responsibility. You cannot object because his new way of life is different from the one he had with you. However, if you discover that he is being ill-treated, you should contact the police or an animal welfare organization.

Many people decide to put a much-loved pony out on loan. With a little forethought, this type of transaction can be very successful. The advantage is that you still retain some control over the pony; and if the new home proves successful the loan might eventually lead to a sale. However, do make certain that your loan agreement covers every contingency, and that both parties fully understand what they have agreed to verbally. It is best to put all the conditions of the loan down in writing and to prepare two copies of the agreement, which are then signed by both parties.

Points to settle are the length of the loan; whether the loan is to include tack and other equipment; who is to be responsible for insuring the pony; paying for his feed, shoeing and veterinary bills. Discuss who makes the decision if, for any reason, the pony has to be humanely destroyed. If you trust the other family, it is better to leave this to them; a pony should not have to suffer unnecessarily because you are away when the decision has to be made.

A PARENT'S INVOLVEMENT

It is inevitable that your child's interest in riding will involve you increasingly as she gets older, even if you have no previous experience of horses. Many parents find that their lives and leisure take on a new dimension when their children take to riding. There are so many ways in which parents can become involved; supervising the care of the pony, driving to and from shows, building show-jumps for the paddock at home, and helping in the organization of the local branch of the Pony Club. Some parents dread the day that their children finally give up riding, but the Pony Club does provide them with the opportunity for continued involvement with horses long after their children have grown up.

Pages 86–7 Unloading. A trailer with a front unloading ramp is an advantage as the pony is able to leave the trailer facing forwards. Take care when leading the pony out that he does not bump against the front bar of the partition.

APPENDIX I
The Pony Club

All young riders, whatever their ability, are well advised to join the Pony Club. This is an organization for children and teenagers, up to the age of twenty-one. It has helped and encouraged many thousands of young pony riders, including many well-known riders who have reached the top of their profession.

The Pony Club was formed in 1929 in the UK, where there are more than 350 branches, with a further 1,500 branches or affiliated clubs in other parts of the world.

Each branch is run by voluntary helpers, headed by a District Commissioner, and organizes a variety of riding activities, both instructional and competitive. These include working rallies, where instruction is given according to a rider's ability; competitions with neighbouring branches; outings to major horse shows; and other activities such as scavenger hunts, quizzes, barbecues and discos.

Most branches run an annual camp where, in addition to learning about pony care and management, members have the chance to train in various competitive forms of riding, such as show-jumping, gymkhana games, cross-country and dressage. Some branches also run teams for specialized events such as tetrathlon (riding, running, swimming and shooting) and polo.

All instruction at working rallies and camps is given by trained instructors. To ensure that good riding standards are maintained, members may take tests, the easiest of which is the D test, and the hardest the A test. Very few reach the latter standard, and those who do usually go on to a career with horses.

The annual subscription is not high, and all young riders derive some benefit from membership, if only the opportunity to make friends among people with the same interests. It also provides access to adults with experience and knowledge of ponies and horses, whose advice you will almost certainly need from time to time.

If you do not know who runs the Pony Club in your area, you should write to the national headquarters (see Address List), who will be able to give you the name and address of your nearest branch.

APPENDIX II
Address list

Britain

Association of British Riding Schools
Chesham House
56 Green End Road
Sawtry
Huntingdon
Cambridgeshire PE17 5UY

British Horse Society *and*
British Show Jumping Association *and*
The Pony Club
British Equestrian Centre
Kenilworth
Warwickshire CV8 2LR

British Show Pony Society
The Croft House
East Road
Oundle
Peterborough
Northamptonshire

Byeways and Bridleways Trust
9 Queen Anne's Gate
Westminster
London SW1

English Riding Holidays and
Trekking Association
Homestead Farm
Charlton Musgrave
Wincanton
Somerset

Horse Rangers Association
The Royal Mews
Hampton Court Palace
East Molesey
Surrey

International League for the Protection
of Horses
67a Camden High Street
London NW1

Irish Horse Board
St Maelruans
Tallaght
County Dublin
Ireland

National Pony Society
Cross-and-Pillory Lane
Alton
Hampshire

Ponies of Britain
Ascot Racecourse
Berkshire

The Pony Club
British Equestrian Centre
Kenilworth
Warwickshire CV8 2LR

Riding for the Disabled Association
Avenue R
National Agricultural Centre
Kenilworth
Warwickshire CV8 2LZ

United States

American Association of Sheriff Posses and
Riding Clubs
8133-B White Settlement Road
Fort Worth
TX 76108

American Horse Council
1700 K Street NW
Washington
DC 20006

American Horse Protection Association
1312 18th Street NW
Washington
DC 20036

American Horse Shows Association
598 Madison Avenue
New York
NY 10022

Pony of the Americas Club Inc
PO Box 1447
Mason City
IA 50401

United States Pony Clubs
303 High Street
West Chester
PA 19380

Canada
Canadian Equestrian Federation
333 River Road
Vanier
ON K1L 8B9

Canadian Pony Society
387 Hay Street
Woodstock
ON N4S 2C5

Australia
Australian Riding Pony Association
Seymour Road
Nar Nar Goon
Victoria

Pony Clubs Association of Western Australia
13 Violet Gardens
Shenton Park
WA 6008

South Australia Horse Society
Fisher Road
Hahndorf
SA 5245

Western Australia Horsemen's Association
50 Bombard Street
Mount Pleasant
WA 6153

South Africa
South African National Equestrian Federation
PO Box 52365
Saxonwold 2132

APPENDIX III

Standard abbreviations used in advertisements

SJ	Show-jumping.
CC or XC	Cross-country.
CT	Combined training.
WHP	Working hunter pony – generally applies to a pony which has been placed in WHP classes. This means that it can clear a course of rustic fences and also has good conformation.
PC	Pony Club.
RC	Riding Club.
PBA	Ponies of Britain Association – the pony is registered with the Association. It suggests a nice-looking pony of mountain and moorland type.
NPS	National Pony Society – as above.
BSPS	British Show Pony Society – the pony has quality and is probably a good candidate for showing classes.
M/M	Mountain and moorland – the pony is a native pony, probably registered with one of the breed societies.
HT	Hunter trials or horse trials.
ODE	One-day event.
TB	Thoroughbred – usually refers to a part-bred or cross-bred (i.e., the pony has Thoroughbred blood).
PoB or POB	Ponies of Britain – usually indicates that the pony has qualified for the Ponies of Britain show at Peterborough (the mecca for showing ponies of all kinds).
BSJA	British Show Jumping Association.
JC	Junior Grade 'C' – one of the BSJA grades. Ponies which jump in affiliated jumping classes have to be registered with the BSJA and be the property of members of the BSJA. Affiliated jumping classes have courses of a certain height which ponies must complete within a specific time limit. Once JC ponies have won a particular amount of prize-money, they are upgraded and can only enter show-jumping competitions open to that grade.
JA	Junior Grade 'A' – the top grade in BSJA jumping ponies.
BHS	British Horse Society.
HIS	Hunter Improvement Society – a society aimed at improving the quality of hunters.
HOYS	Horse of the Year Show – the major show in London, which marks the climax of the season and takes place at Wembley every October.
Sec. A/B/C/D	Registered divisions of the Welsh Pony Society. Section A: limited to mountain ponies not over 12 hh. Section B: ponies 12 to 13.2 hh. Section C: Welsh ponies of cob type. Section D: Welsh cobs.

APPENDIX IV
USA equivalents of terms in common use

Britain	USA
back at the knee	calf kneed
bandages	leg wraps
barking foal	barker
broken wind	heaves
brushing	interfering
caul	sac
cracked heel	scratches; greased heel
cubes	pellets
field	paddock
fortnight	two weeks
girth	cinch; girth
good doer	good keeper
hacking; riding out	pleasure riding; trail riding
halt (long distance rides)	check point
halter	rope halter
headcollar	halter
horse-box	van
laminitis	founder
loose box	box stall
lorry	truck
lucerne	alfalfa
maize	corn
nettlerash	hives
numnah	saddle pad
offset cannons	bench knees
on a sixpence	on a dime
over at the knee	calf kneed
overreach boots	bell boots
paddock	corral
plaits	braids
rein back	back
remove shoes	reset shoes
rise to the trot	post
rosette	ribbons
rug, rugging	blanket, blanketing
sack	feed bag
setfast	tying up; azoturia; Monday morning disease
show schedules	prize lists
sleepy foal	sleeper
society; organization	conference
stable rubber	stable towel
stirrup treads	stirrup pads
tarred road	black top
to rasp teeth/hooves	to float teeth/hooves
travel a horse	truck a horse
wind galls	wind puffs

Index

Page numbers in *italics* refer to illustrations.

J

K

L

M

N

O

P

Q

R

S

T

V

W

Y